Combat and Other Shenanigans

PIERS PLATT

To my wife, who is still putting up with my shenanigans.

CONTENTS

INTRODUCTION

One of the first things a veteran learns when he returns from a combat zone is that war defies easy summary. Upon seeing me for the first time after I had served in Iraq, and after a suitable period of small talk, every one of my civilian friends inevitably asked me what Iraq was like. For all my willingness to share my experiences, I found it nearly impossible to describe it.

"Hot," I would say. "So hot you can't touch the armor of your tank without gloves on."

Which is true, but it doesn't convey the grinding oppression of 130° heat, day after day, what it feels like to sweat through a two-inch thick Kevlar vest in a matter of minutes, or the fact that you have to force yourself to eat despite feeling full from the gallons of water you must drink to survive. So this book is, I hope, a reasonably accurate response to all of those people who asked me what it was like.

The stories in this book are all true, or at least, as close to the truth as my memory allows. However, I changed the majority of names, and certain operational details have likewise been omitted or changed. My apologies to any of my comrades who feel they have been misrepresented, misquoted, or forgotten. My thanks to Joe Comley, John Orbe, and Steve Turner, comrades who helped clarify some stories and technical details, and to Mark Glassman and my father, who agreed to be subjected to painfully early drafts of this book.

While the stories in this book are true, and hopefully paint a better picture of what serving in Iraq was like, any collection of humorous anecdotes about war is – by its nature – woefully incomplete in conveying the true experience of war. For all the absurdity of war, there is exponentially more pain and suffering. Bulldawg Troop lost three of our brothers in Iraq: PFC Owen Witt, PFC Anthony Dixon, and SGT Armando Hernandez. Mere words will never be able to convey the sacrifice they made, as much as their story deserves to be told. There are those of us who left that place and took up our lives again. There are others – far too many others – who will never come home.

i

CHAPTER ONE

"Mushrooms on point!"
-Armor Officer Basic Course 03-04 Troop Motto. Mushrooms, like junior
officers in training, are fed crap and kept in the dark.

I knew that I wanted to join the Army by the time I was in high school. I joined my college's ROTC program partly out of genuine patriotism and a desire to give something back to my country, and partly because I felt like I had something to prove. Although I am extremely grateful for it, I led a privileged childhood – learning Latin and French in private schools, traveling to Europe with my family – and I knew that the rest of my life would probably go just as smoothly. I would go to a good college and get a decent job…and some part of me would always feel like I hadn't really earned any of it. I wanted to force myself out of that comfort zone and test myself in a world where that background was completely irrelevant – where my success or failure was determined by me, and me alone.

As a result, while most of my friends were getting settled into their new jobs after graduating from college, I reported to Fort Knox, just before the invasion of Iraq in March of 2003. Along with the 60 other newly-minted officers in my class, my ROTC training had taught me the fundamentals of leadership and ground warfare tactics; we were at Knox to become tank platoon leaders, to learn how to lead four M1 Abrams into combat. So we spent four months at the United States Armor Center being forged into warriors, soaking in the details of administrative protocols, memo writing, how to

1

inventory equipment, the correct paperwork process for vehicle maintenance, how to write evaluation reports, the disciplinary action process, the evils of venereal diseases (cue 30 minute slideshow of STD-stricken genitalia), how to use PowerPoint, and on Friday afternoons from 4 to 5 p.m., how to lead tanks in actual tactical maneuvers.

No one had bothered to update our curriculum since 1952, so one day we had the pleasure of listening to several lectures on how to socialize with other officers in the Army, including dinner table etiquette, and how to write a proper "thank you" letter. I guess there's been an epidemic of rude Lieutenants ruining dinner parties all over the Army, because our troop commander decided we needed a practical exercise to get that lesson to sink in, and we were all invited to dinner on Saturday at his house. After all the classes, I was expecting it to be a formal affair, but his wife had other plans. In a gesture of protest at the Army for forcing her to feed 60 young men, she handed out paper plates and pointed us at a make-your-own cold cut buffet before disappearing for the evening.

Our troop commander was undoubtedly the worst part of training. A better man might have skimmed through the bullshit with a knowing wink ("I know guys, let's just get it over with and move on to the stuff you care about"), but he made wasting our time into an Olympic sport. He was a military history nut, and while I am, too, that somehow translated into twice the standard amount of homework, and him dragging 60 hung-over Lieutenants around Kentucky's civil war battlefields every other Saturday. He was also a Mormon, which I don't have an issue with, but on several occasions he lectured us on the evils of alcohol, which went over about as well as if we had tried to tell him his religion was a thinly-veiled excuse to have sex with multiple women. One of my classmates, who could play dumb enough to pull it off, brought a bottle of wine to the cold cut dinner party as a gift.

*   *   *

Officer basic training includes five days of field training on the tanks, a series of tactical exercises known as "The Gauntlet." It sounds a lot cooler than it is: considering that each tank is crewed entirely by brand-new Lieutenants, it's a miracle we got the tanks all moving in the right direction. But given how little tactical training we'd had so far, I was looking forward to those five days as the only useful thing that Officer Basic Training included.

In the week leading up to the Gauntlet, I had a few bad nosebleeds – one during a Physical Fitness test, which caused me to finish my 2-mile run with a blood-stained shirt, to the great amusement and cheering of my friends. I was embarrassed, figured I was dehydrated, and shrugged it off with a couple extra glasses of water a day. Several days later, we were driven out to the Gauntlet training area, and my crew was standing around, waiting for our instructor and the tanks to show up, when my buddy Wes pointed to me.

"Dude, Platt – your nose."

I was bleeding, *again*. I wadded a tissue up the offending nostril and tried to laugh it off, annoyed at the inconvenience. But the bleeding wouldn't stop – soon I had soaked through my tissues and was bleeding fairly freely into one of my canteen cups, for lack of a better solution. The instructor soon showed up and whisked me off to the medic area, where they gave me some gauze bandages and had me try all the usual nosebleed tricks. At about the half hour mark they started getting worried (my passing out briefly from blood loss didn't help) – I got an IV drip and a speedy ride to the base hospital. The ER doc on duty told me that the skin inside my nose had been damaged somehow, exposing a vein. He was going to try a special type of bandage, and if that didn't work, cauterizing. All of this sounded fine until he explained that the damaged area was: "way up there."

He took a tongue depressor and a giant tampon-like bandage, and told me I might feel some discomfort, which turned out to be the understatement of the century. He then proceeded to use the tongue depressor to shove the tampon up my nose, to the point where about half of the tongue depressor was up there, too. It felt exactly like someone was jamming a tongue depressor most of the way up my nose. I cursed him loudly and repeatedly, so he added a morphine dose to my IV bag and I fell asleep in the middle of explaining the horrible things I was going to do to him and his family.

When I woke later, he told me that the cauterization was unnecessary, but the trade-off was that I now had to spend the next five days with a tampon up my nose, and in the final blow to my remaining dignity, the tampon bandage even had a string dangling from it, which would be taped awkwardly to my face.

"I can live with that," I told the doctor. "Can I call my unit and get a ride back out to the field now?"

He laughed at me. "No – while that thing is in, you need to keep from aggravating it any further – no tanks, no physical exercise, nothing that could open it up again. You need to keep it in there for five days."

Five days – I would miss all of the field training. On the plus side, if the Iraqi insurgents decided to throw a dinner party, I was ready to politely thank you letter the hell out of them.

CHAPTER TWO

"Tanks are easily identified, easily engaged, much-feared targets which attract all the fire on the battlefield. When all is said and done, a tank is a small steel box crammed with inflammable or explosive substances which is easily converted into a mobile crematorium for its highly skilled crew."
-Brigadier Shelford Bidwell, British military historian

After we graduated from the basic course, each of us received our duty assignment – the combat unit where we would begin serving our four-year active duty commitments. The war in Iraq was supposedly over – President Bush had just pulled his infamous "Mission Accomplished" publicity stunt – but the news reports we saw made it clear that the insurgency was rapidly gaining momentum. So all of us wanted to know whether we had drawn a unit that was already deployed, or whether our unit was simply training at its home base. Some of my friends got assigned to deployed units, and within weeks they, too, were in Iraq. Along with several of my classmates from Fort Knox, I was assigned to the 1st Squadron, 4th Cavalry regiment (better known as 1-4 CAV, or the "Quarterhorse") which was based in Schweinfurt, Germany. The Quarterhorse was part of 1st Infantry Division, the "Big Red One," which had not deployed to Iraq for the initial invasion, but it would be deploying soon.

I had only a dim idea of the difference between a cavalry squadron and a regular armor battalion, but I soon found out: the "Cav" was infinitely cooler, and flaunted that fact at every possible opportunity.

Whereas an armor battalion is made up of three tank companies, each comprised of three tank platoons, a cavalry squadron has three "troops" instead of companies (A, B, and C Troop), each of which contains two tank platoons (made up of four M1 Abrams each) and two scout platoons (made up of six M3 Bradleys – armored vehicles which can also carry several soldiers). In addition, the Quarterhorse also had two troops of Kiowa Warriors: small, lightly armed scout helicopters.

The cocky élan of the cavalry was apparent as soon as I showed up for work on the first day, as the motto painted on our headquarters building proclaimed: "Cavalry is a state of mind." And it was – we called ourselves different things (squadron instead of battalion, troop instead of company, trooper instead of soldier) and set ourselves apart whenever possible. Cavalrymen wear black Stetsons in defiance of Army uniform regulations, decorated with rank insignia, unit crests, and any awards that that trooper may have received. In addition, every cavalryman may earn the right to wear spurs (a throwback to our horse-riding heritage) by participating in a "Spur Ride," a 48 hour test of physical endurance, technical skills, and tactical knowledge, accompanied by a healthy dose of hazing. I earned my spurs a different way: by serving in a cavalry unit in combat.

We were always getting into trouble with the authorities in Schweinfurt, since we were co-located with the 1st Infantry Division's 2nd Brigade Combat Team. Technically, 2nd Brigade is commanded by a full Colonel, who outranks the Lieutenant Colonel in charge of the Quarterhorse. However, since we weren't a part of 2nd Brigade and instead reported directly to the General commanding all of 1st Infantry Division, we weren't subject to the Brigade commander's rules, much to his chagrin. One of his pet peeves was soldiers playing games (flag football, soccer, ultimate frisbee, etc.) during physical training, so a few months before we deployed, he outlawed them across Schweinfurt. We ignored this, naturally, and continued our weekly Lieutenants vs. Captains matches. Invariably, some outraged officer from 2nd Brigade would march up and ask to speak to the senior guy there. Whoever that happened to be would saunter over and listen politely while the new "no games" rule was explained to us.

"Ah, I see. So this is a 1st Infantry Division rule now?"

"No, it's Colonel Dragon's rule for 2nd Brigade."

Smiling: "Ahh…well, here's the thing: we're not in 2nd Brigade, so unless the General says 'no games,' we're gonna keep on playing."

I was soon assigned to lead a tank platoon: 4th or "Green" Platoon in B Troop, the "Bulldawgs." In true Army tradition, my first introduction would be at Physical Training on Monday morning. Physical Training has never been my strong suit – I was skinny enough to not have any issues with push-ups and sit-ups, but running had always been the bane of my existence. Predictably, Monday in 4th Platoon was "long run" day.

I was in pretty good shape, but my two new section sergeants were eager to show me that they could run me into the ground. I hung in there, but only barely, and only because we slowed the pace for a couple of our soldiers who were straggling. I came close to puking twice – which would *not* have been a good start. Throughout the run, Staff Sergeants Peiper and Kean (I didn't get their names until afterwards) harassed and bullied the soldiers like twin sheepdogs, nipping at heels and generally inferring in no uncertain terms that they would prefer to take a bunch of schoolgirls to war rather than the sloppy, overweight, shit-for-brains crew they had been given.

The outgoing platoon leader, Vince Taylor, would be handing things off to me over the coming weeks, before being promoted to take over 1st "Red" Platoon, a scout platoon in the same troop. After we did some cool-down exercises, Taylor introduced me to Kean and Peiper, who would each be commanding one of my four tanks (the other two being commanded by me and my platoon sergeant). Before I could even shake his hand, Staff Sergeant Peiper was giving me a hard time.

"How old are you, sir?"

I grinned, "Twenty-three."

He spat loudly, threw a disgusted look at Kean, and walked off, shaking his head.

"Don't worry about him, sir," Kean smiled warmly, gripping my hand. "As long as you listen to us, we won't let you fuck up too bad."

*   *   *

I was barely done inventorying my new equipment (thank god my training had prepared me for the rigorous challenge of counting wrenches and then putting a check mark on my clipboard), when I had a chance to demonstrate my complete lack of field leadership experience – we were all heading to gunnery training.

Field training is both exhausting and exhilarating, the most fun you can have in the Army under the least comfortable conditions. Over the course of two weeks, we would have to qualify all soldiers on their pistols and rifles, test-fire our tanks, conduct three or four preliminary tank gunnery "Tables," and qualify each tank crew on Table VIII, the final exam of tank crew qualification. Each tank "Table" consists of a series of engagements designed to replicate the different combinations of targets a tank crew could face, escalating in complexity and number of variables involved. These variables include: day and night firing, degraded operations (i.e., the tank has been damaged and is not fully working), firing while stationary and while moving, firing at stationary and moving targets (both troops and vehicles), firing the tank's main gun and three machine guns both individually and simultaneously, and, everyone's least-favorite: firing while in a simulated nuclear/biological/chemical attack scenario, which means wearing a gas mask and protective suit.

Gunnery is rehearsed for hours ahead of time in specially designed simulators, fully operational mockups of tank turrets which include a computer-generated gunnery program, like a video game. The tank commander and his gunner practice the exact engagements they will be facing in Table VIII, for hours on end, until they are functioning as a synchronized team. Nearly as important as actually hitting the targets – which a good gunner can do out to a range of two miles, with the first round almost every single time – is the communication between the two men, known collectively as "fire commands." The rules of fire commands must be followed strictly, otherwise points are deducted from the crew's score. Not only must your crew engage the targets that pop up in the correct order (most dangerous first), the tank commander must quickly and accurately report the results of his engagement following each round, so that, as in actual combat, his troop commander can build an accurate picture of how the fight is developing.

The inside of the tank turret is a white-painted metal box about five feet wide, six feet across, and five feet deep. It can be sealed off from the outside world by closing the two hatches on the roof, but this severely limits how well you can see outside the tank, aside from making it unbearably hot (tanks have no air conditioning). Inside the turret, the tank commander sits on the right, with his gunner immediately in front of and slightly below him, while the loader stands to the left. The fourth man of the crew, the driver, has a separate seat down in the hull of the tank, which is accessible via a hatch on the front slope of the tank.

For their own safety in the cramped confines of the turret, each member of the crew must remain completely focused on and synchronized with the correct sequence of tasks during gunnery. The loader is in the most danger: his job is to open a hydraulic door (which will easily crush his hand when it closes should he be incautious), select the correct round for the target, pull it out of its rack, flip 80 pounds of high explosive end-over-end, ram it into the open breech (being careful to quickly withdraw his arm lest the breech close on his arm), and then flip the main gun's safety off after moving out of the breech's recoil path. Our fastest loaders could accomplish all of this in three seconds flat. Should he fail to clear the recoil path and should the tank commander, being lazy or forgetful, fail to check that the path is clear, nearly a ton of steel will slam into the loader at breakneck speed when the gun fires and the breech slams backward.

The entire crew communicates over their own intercom system which is piped through your helmet's ear-cups and is always live – you just have to talk into the microphone in front of your mouth and the rest of the crew hears you. The ear-cups are active noise reducing, so they minimize the deafening sound of the tank engine and weapons firing, although you can turn this filtering off should you want to hear normally.

In addition to the three other members of his crew talking, a tank commander is also listening to his platoon radio net, which is used for communications between tanks in his platoon alone. Only one person at a time can broadcast on a radio net, but this still adds a second layer of sound if your crew is already talking. Finally, tank commanders will tune their second radio to the troop radio net, which allows vehicles among different platoons in the troop to talk to one another. Layer three! As an added bonus, when enemy contact occurs, the radio nets invariably go nuts with reports and orders, so at the exact moment you want to have a clear head so you can think straight, three different voices are usually yelling in your ears. Turn on two radios and your TV all at once and you'll get a good idea for the kind of skill necessary to be able to filter information from three sets of voices simultaneously.

For tank commanders and gunners, the most nerve-wracking part about gunnery is that your internal microphones are "hot" at all times, meaning the graders watching your performance from the control tower are also listening intently to every word that is spoken in the tank. Every single mistake is recorded, deducted from your score, and later replayed for your benefit at the after action review.

Tank Table VIII includes ten engagements, six during the day, and four at night. The most complex engagement, known to tankers as "The Super Bowl," is fired while the tank is driving, and includes two moving vehicle targets, one stationary vehicle target, and a set of troops. If you fire at the troops first, you fail the engagement. If you fire at the far vehicle or the moving vehicle first, you get points deducted – the nearest stationary vehicle is the most dangerous target, so you should have fired at it first. If you allow any target to drop without hitting it, you get points deducted. If the tank commander says to fire at one thing and the gunner shoots at another, you get a lot of points deducted. To qualify, crews must achieve a passing score of 70 out of 100 on all ten engagements, for a minimum overall score of 700 points out of a possible maximum of 1,000. "Shooting a thousand" is the tanker equivalent of pitching a perfect game, and happens nearly as rarely – a tanker will be extremely lucky to serve on a "1,000" crew just once in a 20-year career. When it happens, the tank commander buys his crewmembers each a case of beer.

Besides often having to sleep on the vehicles or stay up most of the night waiting for our turn on the range, gunnery sucked because of the field rations, which were most often pre-cooked, long shelf-life "meals" reheated in hot water. They were, predictably, disgusting, and only barely palatable with a heavy dose of Tabasco and/or ketchup. Soldiers, however, are nothing if not resourceful, and besides packing bags full of candy, beef jerky, and sodas, we had a secret weapon: Staff Sergeant Peiper had the local bakery trucks on speed dial. Around 11:30 each morning, almost without fail, Peiper could be heard standing on the top of his turret (for better signal), shouting into his cell phone.

"Hans! Ja, ja...hier ist Peiper. Kommen-sie bitte auf Range nummer hundert acht-zehn!"

And ten minutes later, instead of powdered eggs and soggy hash browns, we'd be feasting on hot schnitzel sandwiches with Bavarian pastries for dessert. Even the German employees who ran the ranges (known as "range-meisters") got in on the action, selling Snickers and Schwip-Schwap, a German cola – breakfast of champions.

*   *   *

The majority of our tank gunnery training time was spent in the company of White (2nd) Platoon, our sister tank platoon in Bulldawg Troop. There was a good-natured rivalry between the two platoons, but we got along well. Their platoon leader was Brian Pierce, who had the good fortune to have one of the best platoon sergeants in the squadron, Sergeant First Class Nicholls. Nicholls was a loud-mouthed New Yorker who gave his opinion whether you asked for it or not, and he was invariably right, to the consternation of nearly every officer he served under. He lived and breathed tanks, and was a walking repository of tank technical details, mechanical intricacies, and cavalry lore.

Somehow, Nicholls had acquired a bullhorn which included a siren as part of his personal kit, which he used to great effect throughout field training. Many a napping soldier was rudely awakened with a bullhorn siren in his ear, or an imperious announcement at 6am from the tower overlooking the firing range:

"Wake up, shitheads!"

About halfway through our training, while running a range tower with no adult supervision around, Nicholls had the brilliant idea of blasting the bullhorn's siren sound effect over the range radio, which broadcasts (anonymously) to hundreds of other ranges in the training complex, as well as the Range Control headquarters building. At random intervals, both night and day, the radio would crackle to life and a strident siren would rip out of the radio speakers, immediately followed by increasingly pissed-off orders from Range Control for "whoever it is" to "quit broadcasting the siren."

Because live bullets are being fired, Range Control enforces extremely strict safety procedures, violation of any of which will

11

result in the range being shut down temporarily and the Non-Commissioned Officers (NCOs - sergeants) or officers in charge being "de-certified" (unable to supervise training and continue to run the range). The rules get a bit ridiculous at times, especially in Germany, where following the rules is the national pastime, so decertification happens to nearly everyone at least once during training – I was decertified while leading my very first range after forgetting (sleeping through) some mandatory early morning radio report.

At one point, Nicholls and I were running a range together, he as Range Safety Officer, and me as Range Officer in Charge. Out of the squadron's nearly 30 tanks, just one final tank was left on the range, preparing for its gunnery qualification run. But we were about two minutes away from "dry time" in the afternoon, when the range had to be shut down, and there was no way this tank was going to finish in time. In addition, our medics (who by regulation need to be present every time a tank main gun is fired), had orders to move elsewhere as soon as dry time rolled around. Nicholls was pissed.

"Switch out with me, sir."

"What? Switch out as Range Officer? Why?"

"Because I'm about to get decertified."

It was too deliciously bad to refuse. We switched out (calling it in to Range Control, who maintains a log of who is in what position on which range), meaning that technically, he was now *both* the Range Officer in Charge *and* the Range Safety Officer, which was illegal. It wouldn't take Range Control long to realize that administrative violation, and more importantly, they would *hear* our last tank merrily blasting away during dry time from all the way across the training area. It all came down to whether or not that tank could get enough rounds off before someone from Range Control physically showed up – Nicholls had already turned down the volume on the Range Control radio so we wouldn't hear their inevitable attempts to contact us. The race was on.

For seven glorious minutes, that tank lit up the range. Then, just as the echoes reverberated from the final round, a Range Control van came tearing into the parking lot, and the Range Control NCO hustled out to climb the tower steps. By the time he burst in the door, Nicholls was on the radio already, like the smartass he was, calling in our request to close the range as if he had no idea what had just happened.

Nicholls had served as the squadron Master Gunner several years earlier, charged with overseeing training for all of the squadron's tanks, so he knew all the tricks of the trade. In that role, he had kept a stack of recertification memos already signed by the squadron commander, so that whenever someone was decertified, he could scoot directly over to Range Control and recertify them in a matter of minutes. Once, Range Control showed up on a range he was observing and decertified the Officer in Charge for a totally nitpicky, chickenshit reason, so Nicholls gave the Range Control guy a piece of his mind, which resulted in him being decertified as well, for general rudeness, apparently.

"I'm the squadron Master Gunner!" Nicholls told the man, laughing, "I'll be recertified before you can fucking blink!"

He hopped in his van, hauled ass across the training area to Range Control, and dropped off his recertification memo. The guy there looked at it, confused.

"Uh, you're not decertified..." He told Nicholls.

"I will be," Nicholls replied.

As he walked back out the door, he met the guy who was about to decertify him, and flashed him a shit-eating grin.

*   *   *

Serving under me in 4th Platoon were two outstanding Staff Sergeants, Kean and Peiper. Peiper was my wingman, meaning our tanks – Green 1 (me) and Green 2 (Peiper) – would be operating as a mutually-supporting team during operations. The Army can be a pretty depressing place if you lose your sense of humor, but I soon learned that that would never be a problem with Peiper around. Much of the road network at the training area that year was being repaved, so there were temporary road signs along nearly every road. As we rolled our tanks out of the motor pool and headed for the shooting ranges on the first day, Peiper took the lead, and decided that those temporary road signs made for an excellent training opportunity for his driver. As we approached each sign at about 35 miles per hour, I watched his tank swerve partway off the road, make a minor steering adjustment to line up the road sign with the tank's right-side tread, and then systematically crush it under 70 tons of steel.

Peiper loved his tank more than life itself, and the way he doted on it and tinkered reminded us of Han Solo's relationship with the Millennium Falcon. By the time we left Iraq, that tank had an absurd amount of modifications – all against Army regulations, but brilliantly designed. Peiper built himself a GPS stand in his hatch, which not only held his portable GPS receiver where he could view it easily, but also kept it charged off the tank's batteries. He designed and welded a metal rack for the turret that held extra cans of ammunition within easy reach of both his machine gun and the loader's. At one point, he even wired a police car spotlight to his gun tube, which he found an infrared filter for, so that you could use it as an extra headlight, or make its beam only visible through night vision goggles.

A number of Peiper's "upgrades" were aesthetic in nature. To begin with, the interior of his turret had been literally wall-papered with porn – hundreds of centerfolds had been painstakingly cut and pasted on every available surface. Months later, we were manning a checkpoint in Iraq along with a medic Humvee. One of the medics happened to be a woman, and she wandered up to Peiper's tank after a hot, boring hour of watching the empty road.

"I've never been on a tank, Sergeant...can I see what it's like inside?" She asked.

Peiper was momentarily rendered speechless.

"Um...no?" he said. He and his loader remained planted firmly in their hatches.

Tankers often paint slogans or insignias on their gun-barrels and hatches. Generally, these are badass words or comical phrases starting with the letter of the troop that platoon is in: an "A" Troop tank might have "Assassin" on its barrel, for instance. Peiper chose to meticulously copy a lesser-known SS Panzer Division insignia onto his gun tube, and decorated his hatch with the Wehrmacht's slogan: "Gott mit Uns." Though he was a hardcore history buff, he was no neo-Nazi – it was entirely out of boyish rebelliousness and respect for the legendary prowess of German armored forces. No one picked up on it, of course, until we were out conducting a mission in Iraq and told that several journalists were headed to our location for some interviews in the field.

About five minutes after the call came through, our journalists showed up in a couple of Humvees. We were expecting an ABC

News crew or something, but it turned out they were actually from a toy model magazine that specialized in accurate military replicas – basically they wanted some pictures of our M1 Abrams tanks on actual combat missions to serve as the basis for a new model design. All of which might have been okay, had they not also been German.

There was an awkward moment after we were introduced, standing there in front of his tank, in which Peiper and I shared a long look. Then the escort Humvees rolled back a bit, leaving us alone with the journalists, and one of the Germans, leaning forward and pointing to the gun tube, whispered conspiratorially, "Das ist Waffen SS!?"

Peiper grinned: "Ja, genau." *Exactly.*

The two men burst into laughter. They liked the porn on the inside even more. We gave them a tour of the vehicle, they took pictures from all angles, and gave us their business cards before they left. I haven't been able to find it yet, but Peiper tells me there's a German model set out there of his tank, with our picture on the box – and if you look very closely, you can just make out a strange insignia on the gun tube.

*   *   *

Our gunnery training was my first exposure to an age-old Army institution known as "Private jokes." Practical jokes which take advantage of new soldiers' (Privates) lack of experience and gullibility, Private jokes are an immensely entertaining time-killer for the many "wait" periods of the Army's "hurry up and wait" work rhythm, while also letting the NCOs involved blow off a little steam. They all follow a similar pattern:

1.   Order a Private to complete a task that is either nonsensical or impossible to achieve, but sounds plausible to an inexperienced soldier
2.   Subtly reinforce that this task is critical to the unit's combat effectiveness and by extension, our country's national security
3.   Watch selected Private struggle to understand / interpret his instructions, but brush them off if they request clarifications
4.   Profit as you watch the unfortunate victim attempt to carry out his orders

15

For instance, a Private will be summoned to the NCO's location, and told to check a tank's armor for "soft spots." The Private will be handed a hammer and a can of spray paint and told to circle any spot that sounds suspicious when hit with the hammer. The end result is a bewildered Private and a tank that looks like it has contracted chicken pox.

Otherwise, a Private might be asked to "check the tank's shocks" by jumping up and down on the back deck – an utterly futile action on a 70-ton vehicle. A Private might be handed a plastic bag and told to get an exhaust sample from a tank's engine, which, being a hugely powerful turbine, blows a massive blast of hot air behind the tank. Besides being nearly impossible to hold the bag in the strong exhaust stream, the exhaust is hot enough to melt the bag.

Private jokes can be fairly elaborate, too: while performing maintenance on a radio, a Private will be told to go get a can of "squelch" from the communications shop. "Squelch" is the Army term for the squeaky burst of static-like noise that occurs when you start broadcasting over secure radios. It's a noise, not a physical thing. The victim then reports to the communications NCO, who has not been forewarned, but immediately recognizes the prank:

"Hmmm…squelch? No, we just gave our last can to Charlie Troop. Tell you what, though…I think 601st Maintenance had some last week. Why don't you try them?"

On an especially slow day back in Schweinfurt, Staff Sergeant Kean once had a Private going for nearly six hours on the "can of squelch" trick, including sending him to four different units, which forced him to take the bus between the two different posts in Schweinfurt – *twice*.

Field training provides ample opportunities for pranks; Germany is known for its thick fog in spring and fall, which is just as impenetrable to a tank's thermal sights as it is to normal vision. Therefore, training is often at a standstill for several hours while the fog clears. Each tank range has a series of markers that delineate the left and right boundaries of the range area – the area within which you must fire your rounds. For reasons unknown, these large orange triangles are known as range "fans."

On a particularly foggy morning, Sergeant First Class Nicholls got bored and called two new Privates up to the tower.

"Here's what I need you to do." He paused to let them pull pens and paper out of their cargo pockets to take notes. "Go downrange and turn the range fans on. They are about a thousand yards out, the big orange triangles, you can't miss 'em. There's a little switch on the side, just flip it to 'On' and we'll get this fog blown off. Got it?"

"Yes, Sergeant."

They trotted off, disappearing into the mist, to return about 20 minutes later.

"Sergeant Nicholls?"

"Yeah?"

"Uh…we can't find the switch."

If he'd been really bored, he might have given them more detailed information about the bogus switch and sent them back, but he didn't feel like being too cruel that day.

"Yeah, don't worry about it – we just found the switch in the tower up here. Thanks, though."

Officers aren't exempt from such treatment, either. There is a long-standing tradition in the Army of "rolling up" or hazing new platoon leaders during training. After a long day at one range, as we closed up our tanks and headed to the barracks for some sleep, White Platoon tackled their new Lieutenant, Brian Pierce, who put up a pretty good fight. Staff Sergeant Kean found me at the same time, and warned me to get to the barracks, but a couple of the younger soldiers also found me seconds later and quickly had me on the ground. I fought to get loose, but with five of them on me, I didn't have much of a chance. They quickly had us duct-taped to the point of immobility, and hoisted us each onto a tank main gun tube, dangling underneath by our taped-up arms and legs. After a good five or ten minutes of whacking our butts with hands full of baby powder (which was and still is very confusing to me), they cut us down and made nice. We were both good-natured about it – in an odd way, it's both a way to blow off steam and a bonding moment for the platoon – but other officers have been known to get pretty hot, and have therefore been left trussed up on the gun tube for several hours to cool off.

*   *   *

Later that week Nicholls found another chance to incorporate the range fans into a prank. We were running dry-fire gunnery practice at night – going through all the motions, but not actually shooting real rounds – and Brian Pierce (Nicholls' platoon leader) was about halfway through his run when the Range Control guys showed up. They headed over to the medic vehicle, asked to see their map to the hospital, and then promptly shut the range down and decertified the Range Officer because the map was in the wrong *scale*. The U.S. Army standard map scale is 50,000:1, so it's practically impossible to get hold of maps in the Army at a different scale – but the Range Control handbook specified that all maps to local hospitals must be no larger than 25,000:1 scale. So the range was shut down while they took down names and started the paperwork shuffle to recertify and get the range running again. In the meanwhile, everyone had forgotten to let Brian Pierce and his crew know what the hell was going on, and why they hadn't been given any targets for ten minutes. His first mistake was to radio the tower and let them hear how annoyed he was. Nicholls jumped on it.

"Roger, White One, this is Bulldawg X-Ray. We've been given a 30-minute safety stand-down, cease-fire on the range. They're claiming a tank lased outside the range fans, over."

It's a big no-no to *fire* any weapons outside the range fans, since your tank round might land on another range and kill someone. Doing so results in an immediate safety disqualification for the crew; rumor has it that platoon leaders have been fired for it. But "lasing" (using the tank's laser range-finder to "paint" a target and find its range) is not only totally invisible and impossible to verify, it's also completely harmless – regardless of whether it happens inside or outside the range fans. Brian and his gunner should have realized this and laughed Nicholls off, but it was pretty late at night, and instead they got all riled up and started arguing with him, then arguing with themselves over which of them had lased last, and therefore was responsible. For a solid ten minutes, they were tearing into each other, and every word of it was being broadcast live over the radio to the rest of us up in the tower. Nicholls had them thinking there was some sort of satellite tracking system that had picked them up, and that the squadron commander was on his way down to see what the hell was going on. Brian was livid when they finally let him know it was all a joke.

*　　*　　*

You would think that the tremendous noise and pressure of tank main guns firing would make the shooting ranges in Germany unlikely places to find animals, but you'd be wrong. Not only do the ranges have a large population of deer, but after years of constant exposure to it, those deer have become totally indifferent to live fire training, somewhat in defiance of the rules of natural selection. In an enclosed space – such as between buildings in a city – the shock wave alone from the tank main gun can kill a man, yet these deer wander all over live ranges without a care in the world.

The tank gun sight has a day and night mode, and the gunner may switch between the two as he chooses during the day time (at night, looking through the day sight is useless). In day mode, it is a simple telescopic sight, magnifying objects at distance for greater resolution: it's exactly like looking through powerful binoculars. In night mode, the sight uses infrared thermal imagery, and also magnifies objects at long range. Unlike night-vision goggles, which merely amplify the existing ambient light to create a monochromatic version of what you would see during the daytime, thermal sights actually see in the infrared spectrum, so things can look a bit odd, like a photo negative with really high contrast. Things that give off heat (people, vehicle engines) stick out like sore thumbs, and appear whiter and brighter than cooler background objects like buildings or trees, so we call them "hot spots."

However, as good as our thermal sights are, at 1,000 yards at night, a small herd of deer chewing grass can look *exactly* like the row of heated torso-shaped targets that we use as enemy infantry targets for our machine guns. Accordingly, my gunner and I destroyed six moving tanks, ten stationary tanks, three sets of troops, and four or five deer one evening, much to the delight of the German civilians responsible for operating the range. While my crew and I got an ass-chewing and a 20-minute safety violation stand-down, they grabbed their Tupperware and headed downrange to stock up on some fresh venison. Later that week a particularly tightly-clumped herd looked enough like a vehicle target to fool one tank crew, who sent a main gun round into their midst, with predictably messy results.

*　　　*　　　*

The whole purpose of our live-fire training was to qualify each tank crew on gunnery, in the same way that each individual soldier must qualify with his rifle each year by hitting a minimum number of targets at various ranges. The final exam of tank gunnery is called "Tank Table VIII," and it includes ten engagements, with four taking place at night.

On our Table VIII run, our crew started strong: my gunner, Sergeant Cleary, and I really clicked for the day runs, shooting a near-perfect first six runs. For some reason, we were just a little off on the night runs – we missed a couple crucial targets, and all I could think of as the targets dropped unscathed back out of sight was that goddamn dog from *Duck Hunt* on the old Nintendo, laughing at me. We thought it was close enough that we might not have qualified on our first run (a big deal among tankers), but we actually scored "Superior." It was a tremendous relief – Sergeant Cleary and I had spent countless hours together over the last two months, shooting engagement after engagement on the ranges and simulators, and it felt great to be a fully qualified tank commander after all that work. Cleary had the cigars ready, as was tradition, and he and I lit up outside the range tower after our performance review, ignoring the chill of the Bavarian night.

"Hey, sir."

"Mmm?" I was still messing with the lighter, trying to get my cigar fully lit and hoping Cleary didn't notice my ineptitude.

"Why are you wearing your helmet?"

"Well, I couldn't find my soft cap in the dark. I dunno, I thought I had it in my ruck-sack, but it wasn't there."

I always preferred the baseball-style soft cap over my heavy, uncomfortable Kevlar helmet. Cleary savored his cigar for another long moment, then addressed me again in his Carolina drawl.

"I know where your soft cap is, sir."

I could see his eyes twinkling in the dark now. My face fell, figuring I had lost it somewhere, like an idiot.

"Where?"

He grinned. "About 2,000 meters downrange, sir. You shot it out the gun tube at your long-range moving target."

Though new officers don't know it, shooting the new platoon leader's cap out the main gun during Table VIII is one of the oldest traditions in the armored world. Along with every other platoon leader's gunner, Cleary had taken pains to locate my cap during the smoke break he took before we started our run, had stuffed it into his pocket, and then handed it off to our loader to cram into the gun tube while I was peering into the gunsight. Being new to the tradition, I was still a bit confused.

"You're shitting me, right?"

Cleary laughed. "I wouldn't shit you sir: you're my favorite turd."

CHAPTER THREE

"Warning: due to severe backsplash,
all turds longer than 6 inches should be hand-lowered."
-Graffiti in a porta-john in Kuwait

By early 2004, the situation in Iraq was deteriorating rapidly. The chimera that had been Iraq's weapons of mass destruction had fully evaporated, and many of us in the military felt betrayed by our civilian leadership, though our professional pride prevented us from complaining about it. Although Saddam had been unceremoniously dragged from his hole just a few months before, his capture did nothing to stem the growing sectarian violence, and the winter was marked by increasingly more vicious and deadly bombings across the country. We knew we would be in for a hostile reception wherever 1-4 CAV ended up being stationed. Ostensibly, our mission was to train the new Iraqi Army so that they could secure the country themselves, but we knew that a year was not enough time to build an army from scratch. We were more worried about getting everyone home in one piece.

The final weeks before deployment were consumed with last minute preparations – wills were made out and signed, powers of attorney drawn up for spouses, emergency contact numbers and life insurance forms filled out time and again. As part of our pre-deployment processing, each soldier underwent a thorough physical, which was then topped off with a battery of immunizations. The Army is notorious for losing soldiers' shot records, which they fix by simply repeating any immunizations that aren't on your record, just in case. Thankfully, I had been warned about this, and kept my own copy of my immunization records, so I avoided the double-dose a number of other guys received.

In preparation for living in Iraq for a year, we were injected with a smorgasbord of the usual immunizations for people traveling to developing countries. In addition, the Army also gave us the anthrax and smallpox vaccines, both to protect against possible biological attacks, and because both organisms occur naturally in Iraq as well. The anthrax vaccine is actually a battery of shots given over intervals. In contrast to other vaccines, which usually just sting a little bit and leave you with a small bruise for a day, the anthrax vaccine burns going in, and leaves your arm feeling like it was clubbed with a baseball bat. A small number of people also suffer the unpleasant side effect of having a gland in their armpit swell dramatically for a few days, which gives them the appearance of having a tennis ball under their arm. When we started getting the anthrax battery, there was a major news story about soldiers filing a lawsuit against the Army, alleging that the anthrax vaccine had made them sterile. I don't know what the outcome was, but I decided that a long, sterile life was far preferable to dying from a horrible disease.

For married soldiers looking to maximize their last few intimate moments with their families, the smallpox vaccine is even worse. First, it invariably gives the patient flu-like symptoms for a few days: nausea, weakness, runny nose, fever, the whole deal. Worse, however, it's not a shot – the needle is simply dipped in a petri dish of vaccine, and then stabbed rapidly into your shoulder ten or fifteen times in a row. The resulting wound develops into a pus blister about the size of a dime, which is full of real, live, totally infectious smallpox until it heals. It really turns the ladies on.

*   *   *

We got the call to deploy in early February. The squadron assembled on post, our new desert tan uniforms looking oddly out of place in the frosty German winter. Each of us was absurdly overloaded – on top of our uniform, we wore a Kevlar vest equipped with inch-thick ceramic inserts or "plates" for both the chest and back, and an assortment of modular pouches for ammunition, grenades, and first aid kits. Each man had slung across his chest an M4 or M16 rifle, and most NCOs and officers carried a pistol as well. We wore helmets, assorted gloves, and ballistic eye protection – specially designed safety glasses. This collection tipped the scales at about 30-45 pounds, and added a considerable degree of bulk to one's frame, which took a long time to get used to.

In addition, to bring everything on the required packing list, each man was expected to carry a 50-pound duffle bag full of extra uniforms and miscellaneous equipment, and a 30-pound rucksack filled with more of the same. Each man had at least one other backpack for any other personal items that wouldn't fit into our other bags. Finally, all officers were carrying their laptops (not even combat eliminates the need for paperwork), and certain soldiers were carrying specialty equipment like our new sniper rifles or a medic bag. All told, my gear very nearly outweighed me. After some experimentation, I figured out a way to carry everything at once, though it was a hell of a workout.

Once they had taken accountability of everyone, they marched us over to the squadron hangars, where we would be loading onto buses later that night. There we sat in neat rows on the floor for several hours, while the men with wives and children were able to stay with their families until the buses were near. Then all troopers were told to say goodbye and move into the hangars for good. It was a surprisingly subdued scene – a testament to the courage and strength of the Army wives and children. Goodbyes were said, quietly and tearfully, children hugged one last time, most a little bleary-eyed at the increasingly late hour. It was easier for the younger children, who could not yet comprehend what a 12-month deployment really meant. I avoided the "farewell" area, not wishing to intrude on those private moments, and not at all eager to relive my own farewell experience with my fiancée, who had flown back to the States several weeks earlier.

Buses took us to Nüremberg airport, where our plane waited. Because it would be impossible for the Air Force alone to ferry the masses of troops shuttling in and out of the Iraq, the Army contracts private carriers to handle the overflow. In the Gulf War, they even had to resort to forcing major airline companies to cough up planes to make ends meet, under a compulsive federal system known as the Civilian Reserve Airfleet Program (my favorite government acronym of all time). We would be flying to Kuwait on a rather battered jumbo jet whose paint scheme indicated it was from "World Airways," which seemed to us a bit like getting heart surgery done at WalMart. Our misgivings turned out to be completely justified.

After carefully weighing each of us and our equipment (which quickly devolved into a good-natured competition to see just who had brought the most crap), and after several more hours of waiting, they finally gave us the call to board and began shuttling us to the runway. We boarded the plane via a staircase at the rear, at the foot of which stood a Brigadier General shaking our hands and wishing us luck. On top of the usual nerves, I was starting to get excited: I was about to experience things that might change me forever. If nothing else, I would come back a different person, one who had seen and done things other people only read or dreamed about.

In the post-9/11 world, it was also a particularly odd sensation to carry an assault rifle onto an airliner, the stewardesses smiling while they graciously helped us stow our weapons "in the overhead compartments, or under the seat in front of us." If you think coach seats are cramped, try sitting in them wearing a flak vest. At last we were all crammed aboard and ready for takeoff just before dawn. The plane's captain came on the intercom and gave a little speech, which most of us missed: we were already falling asleep after being up the entire night. We taxied, revved the engines, and hurtled up into the night sky.

I happened to be sitting close to a window, so when one of the port-side engines burst into flame, I saw it immediately, though in my sleep-deprived state, it didn't worry me nearly as much as it should have. The general reaction on board was one of exhausted bemusement:

"Dude, check that shit out!"

"Huh. That's not so good."

"Looks like we're not going to Iraq after all."

"Good – better to die now, I'd hate to get killed eleven months in."

Someone back at Nüremberg had done the math wrong, and the plane was severely overweight. The pilot had been able to get us off the ground in time to avoid clear-cutting the forest at the end of the runway, but only barely, and the stress of generating the necessary thrust had destroyed one of the aging engines, which emitted a 20-

foot-long gout of bright orange flame for half a minute, until the pilot shut it down. The decision was made to land immediately, but for safety reasons (to shed more weight, I suppose), they needed to get rid of most of our fuel first. We spent the next ten minutes dumping fuel over Bavaria, and most of us were back to sleep by the time we touched down again without incident. It was not the proud, heroic march to war I had envisioned, drums pounding and trumpets blaring.

*   *   *

They found us another plane the next day, and we were soon stepping off the plane in sunny, sandy Kuwait. A few days after we arrived in Kuwait, they piled us all into two large buses and drove for several hours into the middle of the desert. The buses stopped next to what initially looked like a Bedouin camp: a cluster of small canvas tents, a handful of rifle ranges and plywood houses, and nothing else in sight for miles. To be fair, though, "nothing in sight for miles" describes most of Kuwait. As we stepped off the buses, a couple of civilians emerged from the tents and gestured for us to take a knee around them. Up close, I revised my assessment – though they were wearing civilian clothes, both men had a quiet intensity and self-confidence that were unmistakable: they were former special operations forces. Characteristically, their welcome brief was short and to the point.

"I'm Bob, and this is Jim. We understand you've all been working on CQB – Close Quarters Battle. We're here to train you on some of the more advanced techniques. Marksmanship first, then we hit the live-fire shoothouses. Everyone grab a can of ammo and let's get going."

We fired more rounds in those three days than I did in the rest of my career combined. Generally, the Army trains soldiers to fire at long ranges, with slow-paced, single shots. Under their expert tutelage, we learned "close quarters marksmanship" – the art of rapidly firing a pair of shots into the center of a target less than 50 yards away, an essential pre-requisite to operations in the tight spaces found inside cities and buildings, where most of our operations would be taking place. In addition, we refined our "room-clearing" skills on mock-up plywood buildings, running scenarios of varied complexities again and again until they became second nature.

One evening we practiced night firing – both shooting with our barrel-mounted flashlights to illuminate the target, and shooting with night vision goggles on. Night firing is far more difficult than normal daytime shooting, but on this particular night, the weather upped the ante by whipping a sustained sand-storm through the area. It was nasty, to say the least: even with goggles and a scarf, the sand worked its way into our throats and eyes, stinging and scratching incessantly, and reducing visibility in the dark to nearly nothing. But one day soon we might need to fight in these conditions, so we pressed on. The M4 rifle is a reliable weapon when cleaned and lightly oiled, but it does not function smoothly with sand in its guts, as we soon discovered. There was no way to keep the sand out, however, so by the end of the night, we were all experts in fixing malfunctions on our weapons, quickly and thoroughly, and by blind feel alone. Such training does wonders for the confidence level of soldiers.

Not only was the training realistic and demanding, it was a hell of a lot of fun, because the instructors made it so. They abolished all of the lock-step rules and procedures which make regular Army shooting such a chore, and just got down to the business of laying steel downrange. One of our soldiers was having trouble getting his sight zeroed in, his rounds landing everywhere on his target except the center-of-mass ring. As the rest of us finished up, we could tell he was nearing the limit of his patience.

"Hold on," Bob said, taking his rifle, "Let me check it."

He assumed an odd, cross-legged seated stance I had never before seen, cradled the rifle to his chest, and blew off ten rounds in a few seconds flat. All ten shots were tightly clustered in the target's "head."

"Nope, she's shooting straight," Bob observed mildly. "We just gotta get it adjusted to where you're aiming."

He handed the weapon back, walked down the range, and knelt down two feet to the right of the target.

"Okay," he yelled. "Go ahead. Shoot, and I'll walk you in."

To the rest of us, brought up on ranges where it was a cardinal sin for anyone to walk in front of the shooting line while there were loaded weapons anywhere in the vicinity, this was about the coolest, ballsiest thing *ever*. With more than a little trepidation, the trooper got back into the firing position and hesitantly fired off three rounds into the target.

"Okay, adjust your sight down two notches."

He did, and fired three more rounds into the paper next to Bob. Bob glanced at the paper again, and adjusted him left one notch. All three rounds landed in the bulls-eye. We nicknamed Bob "Crazy Motherfucker" for the rest of our time there, though no one had the guts to call him that to his face.

*   *   *

After several more weeks in Kuwait, our HETs (Heavy Equipment Transporters) arrived for the journey up to our area of operations north of Baghdad. HETs are massive armored Mack trucks with a trailer that can carry any Army vehicle, including our tanks. They help save both fuel (since an M1 Abrams burns about a gallon of fuel every mile) and wear and tear on the tanks, which require an ungodly amount of maintenance to keep them operational. I'm sure there's an official study out there somewhere about how many man-hours it takes to keep a tank up and running, but I would guess it's almost a one-to-one ratio of operational time to maintenance time.

We would be riding in our vehicles, on top of the HETs, and though our tanks would be chained down, turrets secured and engines off, we had every intention of firing them up and busting those chains the moment we came into enemy contact. With our entry into Iraq itself imminent, everyone's nerves were frayed – tempers were shorter, smiles were tighter, and there was a lot of loud back-slapping and machismo to cover our anxiety. We had become acclimatized to the desert, to a certain degree – to the heat and dust, and the bitterly cold nights – but the novelty of Kuwait had worn off. We were eager to go north, to start getting our tour over with, but I for one felt a growing knot in my belly, and sleep came only sporadically for the last few nights.

On the final morning in Kuwait we took a platoon picture in the sand of the motor pool, some mugging for the camera, others sober and unsmiling. I gave one final safety brief, stressing the importance of vigilance at all times, and what the medical evacuation plan was. I'm not religious, or at least, not in a conventional way, but as I watched my men head off to their tanks, I prayed silently that we would all be back there in 12 months' time, together and in one piece. Then I climbed up into my turret, pulled my helmet on, and placed my rifle beside me.

Sergeant First Class Nicholls started us off on the right foot. On a dare, as we rolled out in a mass of dust and creaking axles, he was standing on the turret of his tank, which is known as "turret-surfing." Turret-surfing is sternly prohibited for safety reasons, but Nicholls was upping the ante by keeping his balance while also performing the "monkey-fucker." The monkey-fucker is a diabolically painful lower body physical exercise which involves standing with legs shoulder-width apart, reaching through your legs to grab hold of the back of your ankles, and then rapidly thrusting your butt up and down in a lewd squatting motion. It is traditionally accompanied with shouts of "fuck that monkey!" and ape-like screeching sounds.

The rest of the ride through Kuwait was without incident – we saw some camels, a few Bedouin, sand, sand and more sand, and finally pulled into a small encampment just south of the Iraqi border, where we would camp the night. Incredibly, they had a Pizza Hut® there, which we all took full advantage of, knowing our food quality was about to take a sharp down-turn.

We entered Iraq just after dawn on the second day of our convoy north. There was no customs house or border gate, not even a sign ("Welcome to Iraq, the Cradle of Civilization!"), only a series of tall earthen berms running perpendicular to the highway in either direction, relics of the Gulf War. I wasn't even sure we had crossed into Iraq until Staff Sergeant Kean (who had been a tank driver back in 1991 on Schwarzkopf's famous "Hail Mary" flanking maneuver) called up over the radio:

"I never wanted to come back to this fucking place."

I locked and loaded my rifle and the .50 cal machine gun, then ducked my head inside to ensure that Sergeant Cleary was loading his own machine gun in the gunner's hole. There were a few comments over the radio about "staying sharp" and things along those lines, but I refrained from sending them along to my platoon, figuring that the majority of us were in a combat zone for the first time, and would need no such reminders. I felt a rush of fear tinged with excitement myself, though the lack of fanfare at the border and the miles of empty desert stretching in each direction made it hard to get too worked up.

The day plodded on, and eventually we began to see signs of life – green patches in the desert, palm trees, scattered mud buildings, dogs, goats, and children. They ran, barefoot, along the side of road as we thundered past, some smiling and waving, others somberly making odd gestures which we later learned was their way of begging for food. We were too new to throw them anything, not knowing what rules we might be breaking, what obscure code of guerrilla warfare might be violated. Some troopers waved back, others ignored them. We all scanned the sides of the road endlessly, sweeping our eyes over lumps and bumps, trash and debris, anything that could conceal an improvised explosive device (IED). They had given us a brief class in Kuwait on some of the lessons learned about IEDs in Iraq, which, at the time, were a relatively recent addition to the insurgent arsenal. A month or so before our arrival, the insurgents had started "daisy-chaining" the bombs: linking multiple bombs in large strands to hit several vehicles at once. The instructors also made it clear to us that any vehicle – even the vaunted M1 Abrams tank – could be destroyed by an IED. It wasn't much of a protective strategy, but they counseled us to be vigilant, to project to all observers an air of hair-trigger readiness, and to move fast, no matter what. Our HETs were certainly hauling ass, pushing 60 mph on the dusty highway.

Mid-way through the first afternoon we had our first introduction to the brutally low value of life in Iraq. Inexplicably, several trucks ahead of me, an Iraqi man decided he needed to cross the road. He was watching our trucks closely as we barreled along, but as he was timing his dash across, an Iraqi truck shot out of the thick dust going in the opposite direction, and slammed directly into the man, tossing him like a rag doll. There was already a large slick of crimson blood in the road in the second or two it took my truck to roll past the accident. The Iraqi truck that had hit him didn't even slow down. We were shocked, and were discussing calling a halt over the radio, but one of our medics had gotten a good look at the man as he passed, and assured us there was nothing he could do.

Later that afternoon, we had our first experience with an IED traffic jam – one had been discovered a mile or so ahead of us, so we were halted at a safe distance while the local unit called in EOD (Explosive Ordnance Disposal – the bomb squad). After half an hour, we heard a blast, saw the column of smoke rising, and then simply started driving again. I hoped every future encounter would be so easy.

The Army doesn't stop convoys for bathroom breaks, so everyone was urinating in empty water bottles on the vehicles. Midway through the first day, Vince Taylor and his gunner were standing in the hatches of their Bradley Fighting Vehicle when they felt what they thought was a drizzle of rain. They looked up: blue sky, not a hint of cloud. Puzzled, they began searching for the source of the moisture. Then they saw the soldier in the passenger seat of their HET emptying a bottle of piss out his window. Driving at 60 mph, the spray from the bottle was blowing right back in their faces. While his gunner retched over the side of the Bradley, Vince gave the man an earful over the radio before ducking down into his turret to clean himself off with baby wipes as best as he could.

On the third day we traversed Baghdad. The terrain had gradually shifted during the morning, as we left the great southern deserts behind and emerged into the region supported by the Tigris and Euphrates rivers. Sand had given way to thick scrub grass and bushes, and stands of palm trees began to appear as well. On either side of the highway, somewhat concealed amongst the trees, we saw more and more destroyed Iraqi vehicles, though from which war we did not know. We even saw a Russian-made T-72 tank that had been flipped upside down onto its turret – I wondered what cataclysmic weapon had caused such a result.

We were all excited to see Baghdad, if only for a change of pace from the featureless desert of the day before, though we didn't pass anything recognizable as a landmark in the city. Instead, Baghdad revealed itself to be a slum city stretching endlessly in every direction – there were empty lots piled high with trash right next to people's houses, and it looked as if someone had decided to throw up some ramshackle cement buildings in the midst of a dump. The highway was clogged with an enormous amount of rusty, secondhand cars, and the complete lack of traffic signals meant that the driving conditions were pure chaos.

*   *   *

Our final destination was a Forward Operating Base (FOB) called FOB Mackenzie, a bombed-out Iraqi air base in the desert east of Samarra. The final road march to Mackenzie was both hectic and nerve-wracking. We crossed the Tigris over a pair of tall bridges and entered the southern part of the town of Ad Duluiyah. The town was thick with low-slung power lines, some of which sparked brightly when our vehicle antennas hit them. Still others were low enough that we had to duck down in our turrets to avoid them. Later, we learned that a Bradley commander had been killed by just such a wire a few months before, electrocuted in his hatch when he failed to see the power line ahead of him. The buildings were tight along the road, balconies and rooftops perched just above us on either side, perfect for a would-be attacker, and between ducking under wires and trying to cover every rooftop I could see with my rifle, I worked up quite a sweat. At last we were through the far side of the town, and the HETs picked up steam for the final few miles to the front gate.

Forward Operating Base Mackenzie was several miles north of town, but close enough to be within insurgent mortar range, happily. Despite being only a few miles away from the Tigris, it was far enough north to be outside the green belt of vegetation that hugs the river's banks. A roughly rectangular patch of sand and cement runways about two miles square, the FOB was surrounded by an earthen berm topped with razor wire, and looked out into completely empty desert in all directions. About ten or fifteen large cement bunkers were peppered around the installation, and huge domed aircraft hangars marked the ends of each runway, each sporting a massive hole from U.S. Air Force precision munitions. The whole place was so dusty and depressing, I half-expected a Jawa sandcrawler to appear over the berm.

At Mackenzie we met up with the units from 4th Infantry Division that we were meant to relieve, who were charged with getting us familiar with the area of operations before they went home. After a few briefings from their outgoing officers, I was told to ride with a reconnaissance platoon to see how they ran patrols. One of the things I had told my fiancée to try to console her over my upcoming deployment was that I would be going to battle in an M1 Abrams tank, the most well-protected vehicle in existence. So of course, my first patrol in Iraq turned out to be in a Humvee with fiberglass sides and the doors removed. It looked like it might be a short tour after all.

I got over my fears quickly, and even enjoyed the feel of the cool dusk breeze coming through the doorframe, and the excitement of speeding along the highway without doors. Our mission was to conduct reconnaissance of a large area south of the Jabal Hamrin ridge, a towering razorback of stone running east and south toward the Iranian border, which marked the northern boundary of the Squadron's territory. Lately, insurgents had figured out an innovative way to fire Russian SA-8 anti-aircraft missiles from this area towards our Division Headquarters, located in Saddam's old Tikrit palace complex. An Air Force jet the previous night had spotted some suspicious Bedouin tents in the area and requested a ground reconnaissance to check them out.

It meant covering a lot of ground, all of which was largely uninhabited desert or sparse grasslands. We saw nothing other than grass and dirt for several hours, until we crested a small rise just after midnight and the Jabal Hamrin ridgeline came into view in the moonlit distance. It was a jagged, rocky spine, looking oddly out of place in the desert. On the near side of the ridge there was an oil refinery, which spouted a tongue of flame from one of its smokestacks. The flame was bright enough, even from several miles off, to light the surrounding area with a campfire-like glow. Several hundred yards in front of us was the cluster of cramped Bedouin tents the jet had spotted.

The reconnaissance Lieutenant laughed: "Yeah, way to go, Air Force."

"What?" I asked.

"Have you ever seen an SA-8?"

"No," I admitted.

He smiled. "It's over 10 feet long. It wouldn't even fit in one of those tents. The Bedouin don't give a shit about us, anyway – they're far more interested in their goats. Ah, fuck it – let's go check it out."

We rolled down to the tents and the platoon climbed lazily out of the Humvees, the vehicles arranged in a loose circle around the tents for security. The Bedouins had heard us coming, of course – their dogs had given them plenty of warning. A small man greeted us outside the largest tent, smiling toothlessly. The platoon leader explained his intentions through charades while a couple of his soldiers ambled into the tent, weapons slung, showing no anxiety or concern whatsoever. They popped out a minute later, and an NCO walked up to the two of us and the Iraqi.

"Nothing, sir – guy's got an ancient bolt-action rifle, but that's it."
We climbed back into the Humvees and headed back to the FOB.
Hell, I thought. *This war stuff is easy.*

*   *   *

I would soon get to know that area very well. Soon after our 4th
Infantry Division predecessors headed home and left us in charge, we
received our first mission as a troop: we would conduct a thorough
reconnaissance of the area south of that same Jabal Hamrin ridge –
gather intelligence, basically, about what was up there, who lived
there, whether they were friendly, neutral, or hostile, etc. The scouts
would be responsible for covering the most ground, while the tanks
would set up a series of observation posts watching the roads, and
traffic control points (checkpoints or roadblocks that allow soldiers
to search vehicles) to ensure no insurgents were moving weapons
into or out of the area.

That might have been an important mission in your normal
bustling Iraqi town, but we were conducting it in Iraq's equivalent of
Nebraska: 130 cavalrymen in the world's most advanced and lethal
vehicles patrolling rolling grasslands populated by perhaps 20 goat
farmers. We soon realized our mission was just a training exercise
for our new commanding officer, who had taken command *after* we
had completed all of our critical training in Germany, following the
Army's usual sound staffing logic.

We spent five days out there letting our commander "take off the
training wheels," and our biggest accomplishment was finding what
can only be described as an ammunition junk heap: ancient artillery
rounds rusting in the heat, scattered willy-nilly over a square mile.
We had no idea how it got there ("You want me to just dump all
these rounds in the middle of a field?" "Yes, but not in one big pile
– put them all over the place."), but one of the other platoons would
later spend several months guarding that ammo dump, to their
chagrin and eternal boredom.

After hours of nervous anticipation, worrying about my qualities
as a leader and my ability to make decisions under fire, I was finally
faced with leading my first combat mission, on my own. I spent
hours planning it, and agonizing over contingency plans, risk
assessments, and the like. Then we rehearsed every stage of the

operation several times. At last, we rolled out and established our checkpoint…on a one-lane road, with miles of grass and not a single car in sight. And then we waited.

And waited.

Finally, six tedious hours after we arrived, a lone car approached the checkpoint.

"Okay, guys – just like we rehearsed," I called out, uneasily. My heartbeat quickened.

The car pulled in closer and stopped as directed, heavy weapons covering it from all angles. During training, my NCOs had correctly stressed the need for aggressive, authoritative behavior while running the checkpoint, in order to establish full control over the civilians being searched, and Staff Sergeant Peiper demonstrated this by bellowing at the guy to shut off the car and step outside. I'm sure he didn't speak English, but he fully understood what was needed. He shut off and we waited with breath held, fingers near triggers, as our first Iraqi civilian stepped out of his car. He was piss-drunk.

We were done searching the car in about two minutes, including checking the engine block and trunk, and passing the search mirror under the under-carriage as well. Meanwhile, our lush had tried to hug several soldiers, much to their amusement. Laughing, we pushed him back into his pickup, and he drove off in a more or less straight line after shaking several more soldiers' hands. His was the only car we saw during the eight hour mission.

*   *   *

One afternoon, while the troop rested between "missions" in our assembly area, we got word that a Brigadier General from Division staff was coming to visit. In Iraq, Blackhawk helicopters serve two roles: as medical evacuation (medevac) birds for wounded soldiers, and as air-taxis for the exclusive use of "brass" (senior officers). The General would be flying in on his pair of choppers to observe what operations we were conducting, which was ironic, considering we weren't doing anything useful and we knew it. More importantly, his impending arrival caused our troop leadership to rush to reinstate discipline measures which had slackened somewhat given the distinct lack of enemy presence in the area.

On orders from the troop commander, and accompanied by much

grumbling and eye-rolling, we all pulled back on our Kevlar vests and helmets, sleeping soldiers were kicked awake and hustled into the vehicles to nap out of sight, and trash bags were tucked away. Minutes later, the choppers thundered in overhead, hovered, and made a roaring landing amidst their swirling rotor wash.

Our troop assembly area was a rough circle, several hundred meters in diameter, with each platoon's vehicles arrayed in an arc covering a quadrant of the circle. There were, therefore, nine tanks and 13 Bradleys in a loose ring around the command vehicles in the center, no less than 40 medium and heavy machine guns all pointed outwards (at an empty grass plain), to say nothing of the vehicles' main guns. If you had rounded up all the insurgents in Iraq and forced them to attack us at the same time, not one of them would have been able to make it alive into our perimeter. The White House isn't as well protected as that small circle of grass was.

Regardless, when the General stepped off his bird, six Military Policemen carrying submachine guns strode off the other chopper, and immediately formed a neat circle of bodyguards around the general, weapons at the ready, eyes scanning aggressively. I guess they were still getting used to operating in a combat zone. To show his disdain for these rear-echelon idiots – and authority in general – Sergeant First Class Nicholls walked off into the grass and proceeded to take a leisurely shit while reading a magazine, in plain view of the command vehicles.

Amidst the boredom of watching nothing in the middle of nowhere all day out on the Jabal Hamrin, the arrival of our first set of care packages from home caused quite a stir. Between my fiancée and my mother, I managed to receive no less than 15 boxes in that first round, and the mail runs in the future never slackened much from that amazing pace. I had enlisted their help beforehand to send me packages for the platoon, knowing that not all of my soldiers would be lucky enough to call on such dedicated support, but they went above and beyond anything I had imagined.

In a riot of cardboard and bubble wrap, we broke out bags of chips, cookies, gum, cigarettes, books, toiletries, magazines, even dental tools for cleaning those tough-to-reach nooks inside weapons. I don't know what winning the lottery feels like, but I think I have a good idea. Throughout the rotation, I received countless packages, and a fair number from people I had never met before, who heard about my platoon secondhand and wanted to do something to support us. To all of them, and to anyone who has sent anything to troops in combat, even a simple letter of thanks, thank you. Knowing that he is appreciated is invaluable to a deployed soldier, and can be the difference between depression and determination.

*   *   *

The next day, Squadron headquarters raised us on the radio, and ordered us back to FOB Mackenzie. Bulldawg Troop's primary mission in Iraq was to serve as the 1st Infantry Division reserve element, an armored "ace in the hole" that they could call on as necessary to assist units that found themselves the focus of too much insurgent attention. Frankly, we were a bit surprised: we had only been in theater for a handful of weeks…was Division already calling for its reserve? However, I was excited to be heading back to civilization – some guys love being in the field and living on the tanks, but I've always been a bigger fan of air conditioning, showers, and beds. I was less excited to be heading somewhere that would invariably be more dangerous than miles of grassland with a few drunken Iraqis, however.

For the trip back, we split our convoy into two, and I had the good fortune to be in the first convoy, leaving immediately after we finished refueling. We made the journey back to Mackenzie in a little over an hour, skirting Samarra, with its sparkling golden-domed mosque, before going flat-out across the open desert and pulling into the FOB. Brian Pierce would be commanding the second convoy, which left after us – one of his tanks needed to undergo some maintenance first. The original plan was that he would stay behind overnight to give them time to get the maintenance done, but orders came down from Division to get moving, so they patched up the tank as best they could and hit the road.

Brian's epic convoy became something of a legend over the next few months. From the start, they were plagued with maintenance issues. The maintenance team's tracked vehicle started hemorrhaging oil, which they remedied by collecting oil from the rest of the vehicles in the convoy, even borrowing some from another friendly unit on patrol that they passed en route. The leaking continued, however, and soon Sergeant First Class Peterson (our mortars platoon sergeant) had to take two of his Humvees and drive to a nearby base to stock up on more oil, then catch back up to the armored vehicles.

Next to break down was a Red Platoon Bradley, which simply ground to a halt. After tinkering with it for a little while, the mechanics determined it had officially "shit the bed" and was not going to start again without a major overhaul. It was hooked up to another Bradley to be towed, and they continued on. Then Brian's tank broke down. Again they halted for a short while to see if it could be easily fixed (it couldn't), then they hooked it to another tank and continued on. They had barely covered 20 miles at this point.

A few miles north of Samarra, the lead vehicle in the convoy then took a wrong turn, turning onto the first of two parallel roads. They soon realized they were on the wrong road, and what's more, this was a dead-end road with no way to reach the correct road. Rather than turn everyone around (a laborious procedure for long convoys, especially when towing vehicles), Brian decided to see if an overland route between the two roads could be found, and he sent one of the Bradleys south to see if they could find such a route. The rest of the convoy halted in place. And then Brian's tank caught fire.

When you tow a tank with another tank there is one absolutely critical piece of equipment, other than a towbar or tow cables: a heat shield. This is a large iron box that sits over the towing tank's exhaust and redirects that blazingly hot air harmlessly upwards, rather than blowing directly onto the tank being towed behind it. Unfortunately, this convoy had no heat shields, and so they had jury-rigged a piece of the tank's armor in its place. The armor had slipped, however, and had spent the last half hour directing scalding hot exhaust into Brian's bustle rack, the back of the turret where the crew stores their bags and personal gear. At a certain point, the heat reached spontaneous combustion levels, and the entire crew's uniforms, underwear, spare equipment, CDs, books, food, and other personal items burst lustily into flame.

They expended several fire extinguishers to no avail, and finally got the fire out with the help of a local farmer passing muddy irrigation water to them via a bucket. Around this time, the Bradley sent out on reconnaissance returned, having failed to find a route south – there were irrigation canals blocking the way. Wet and smoke-stained, Brian got the convoy turned around, nearly getting a vehicle stuck in the process, and they resumed their journey. At this point, they had been on the road for several hours already, and they were still barely a quarter of the way to Mackenzie. At his wit's end, Brian got on the radio.

"I'd like to meet the jackass that thought this would be a good idea."

One of the Privates in the troop, a tank driver who had been nicknamed "Skeeter," seized this opportunity to twist the knife a little. He flipped his radio over to broadcast and answered right back, pretending to be Major General Batiste (the 1st Infantry Division commander):

"This is Danger 6 on your troop net. I'm the jackass that thought it was a good idea, *Lieutenant*. Meet me on the ground when you reach FOB Mackenzie. Danger 6, out."

Normally, this would have been immediately discredited as bullshit and met with a good laugh all around, but at that exact moment, two Blackhawks flew past the convoy, heading roughly towards Mackenzie. Those choppers suddenly made it entirely plausible that the Division Commander had heard his outburst. Brian didn't answer the radio, but he did sweat it out the rest of the ride back, wondering if his luck was so bad that General Batiste had been on one of those helicopters, and had randomly been eavesdropping on the Bulldawg Troop net, which some senior officers are known to do just to keep units on their toes. I'd like to be able to say they made it back without incident from there, but half a mile shy of the entrance to FOB Mackenzie, another of the tanks ran out of gas.

CHAPTER FOUR

"Fuck, it's hot.
I'm sweating more than a pregnant nun at Confession."
-*Staff Sergeant Peiper*

Our urgent mission from Division was to relieve an infantry battalion at FOB Normandy in Muqdadiyah, who were in turn being sent south to help fight Shiite cleric Moqtada al Sadr and his rogue militia. On the way there, however, my tank broke down, so while the rest of the troop continued on, Staff Sergeant Peiper and I stopped at a large FOB to rest overnight and then try to repair my tank before continuing on to our final destination. In the morning, Peiper and I made our way to the chow hall for breakfast before seeing to the tanks.

FOB Warhorse was not a "combat" FOB: at the time it was a brigade headquarters and logistical base, so most of the personnel there were service or support types, and they had the luxury of a civilian-run dining facility. We were just sitting down to eat a fantastically lavish breakfast spread worthy of the Ritz when the FOB started to take incoming enemy mortar fire, and a heavy explosion rattled the massive tent. Back at FOB Mackenzie, mortar attacks had been relatively frequent – an unpleasant experience, but we had quickly come to think of them as just another annoyance of Iraq. From time to time, insurgent mortar teams would lob a few rounds inside the perimeter; usually no one was hurt, so we generally ignored them. It was partly an acceptance of the grim reality that there was

40

little we could have done to protect ourselves, and partly dumb Army machismo to pretend to be bored or indifferent in the face of fire. I soon learned to sleep through such attacks, but that was mainly due to lack of sleep in general.

The soldiers at Warhorse, however, had not reached this stage of nonchalance. Like cockroaches when the kitchen light comes on, the tent erupted into frenzied activity, as people crouched under tables (news flash: plastic picnic tables do not stop mortar rounds) and dropped their trays in a dead sprint for the bunkers outside. Peiper and I were amused, to say the least, but as we continued our eggs and bacon a harried-looking Captain skidded to a halt next to us and, gasping, ordered us outside to the safety of one of the bunkers.

"Seriously, sir?" I asked, without thinking. I was about to get a severe ass-chewing, but before he could respond, Peiper saved me with a quick redirect.

"Can we bring our food, sir?"

As it turns out, we could not. Luckily, though, that Captain was more worried about getting under cover than taking our names down and reporting us for being wise-asses and ignoring FOB rules. But the civilians running the dining facility, god bless those war-profiteering bastards, had plenty more hot eggs and bacon waiting when the "All Clear" siren sounded and we filed back inside.

*   *   *

We spent two days working on my tank at Warhorse, and then made the final trip on to Muqdadiyah, a large town on the eastern edge of Iraq, not far from the Iranian border. While all Forward Operating Bases share some similarities, each has its own distinct personality. FOB Normandy felt like a military ghost town. Scraggly trees lined the wide boulevards, dry grass poked through the paving stones of walkways, and shattered windows filled rundown barracks buildings. Normandy was a former Iraqi base for a large mechanized unit, and accordingly, it had a giant motor pool full of vintage armored vehicles of every size, type, and nationality imaginable. To tankers trained for hours on foreign vehicle recognition techniques, it was like a huge *Trivial Pursuit* game. One afternoon soon after we arrived, we explored the motor pool and identified Russian tanks and personnel carriers, French and German vehicles, even one or two

British tanks. Some of them even looked to be nearly operational.

Normandy also contained a shocking amount of serviceable weapons and ordnance stashed in hundreds of bunkers lining its perimeter. While there, our troop scavenged at least six or seven extra machine guns from the abandoned Iraqi armories, which we mounted on the extra Humvees we had been assigned in Iraq. While visiting our soldiers during one perimeter guard duty shift, Peiper, Kean and I also took the opportunity to poke around some of the ammunition bunkers.

Each bunker was lined floor-to-ceiling with rack upon rack of 155mm artillery shells, each nearly a hundred pounds of steel and high explosive, tens of thousands of them filling a bunker. There was enough ordnance on that small base to level Manhattan. It was both awe-inspiring and terrifying to walk amongst the racks of dark green shells, stretching away in every direction in the dark like a grisly wine cellar. Peiper was inspecting a crate of anti-personnel mines when I noticed writing on the stack of rounds closest to me. I shone my flashlight on it. Beneath crudely painted Arabic figures the metal was clearly stamped:

"ROUND, ARTILLERY: 155MM"

Many of the IEDs we feared so much featured artillery rounds made in the U.S.A.

Our living arrangements at Normandy were the worst we had so far experienced in Iraq. We settled into a series of ancient cement bungalows, formerly Iraqi army barracks. The windows and doors were all long gone, and until we got a generator about a week later, we were without lights and power as well. Thankfully, it was still early spring and the nights were cool, though we all realized the necessity of using our mosquito nets about an hour into the first bug-filled night. The showers in our area were all broken, too, so the stop-gap solution until something else could be arranged was the "water bottle method" – take three liters of bottled water, lay them in the sun for an hour or so, then hit the showers. Bottle one would get you partly damp, enough to work up something approaching a lather, at least, and then bottles two and three would get you mostly rinsed off. I'll never take water pressure for granted again.

Normandy was also our introduction to that most feared and loathed of all Iraqi institutions: the burn-shitter. There were three tiers of toilets in Iraq: you had your luxury model, exclusive to large, permanent posts, which consists of a trailer with stalls, porcelain toilets that actually flush, lights, air conditioning, mirrors, and sinks. On the next rung down was the run-of-the-mill porta-john, which can be found at any construction site or rock concert in America. The Iraq versions were little different, except that 130° heat did not mix well with dark green, windowless plastic boxes filled with chemical fumes and raw sewage. At the very bottom of the scale was the burn-shitter. Burn-shitters were constructed from plywood in the traditional out-house style. Instead of being poised over a deep pit, however, you do your business into a 55-gallon steel drum that had been cut in half and filled with a few inches of diesel fuel.

Putting a burn-shitter to use was extremely unpleasant. They smelled horrendous, because even diesel couldn't nullify the stench of human waste that had accumulated over several days of use. They also attracted any fly in a three-mile radius, which meant that your butt, poking through the wooden seat hole, was exposed to the swarm of flies who had been feeding on the sewage below. Taking a sweaty, stinky crap with flies tickling your sphincter was almost as bad as it could get. I say "almost," because the only thing worse than crapping in a burn-shitter was emptying one. If at all possible, this daily duty was reserved as a disciplinary punishment. The victim got hold of the thickest pair of gloves he could find, covered his nose and mouth with a scarf, t-shirt, or surgical mask, and literally burned the shit, stoking it with a long stick or rake. Because the waste was a mixture of fluids and solids, it didn't burn well or quickly, and was notably smoky. The smell was indescribable, and permeated everything around it, especially the unlucky soldier tending the fire. Who then had to rinse off using only plastic water bottles.

*   *   *

When we weren't burning shit, we were handling the unpleasant duty of clearing the roads through Muqdadiyah twice daily to protect convoys from IED attacks. Route clearance consists of driving slowly along the main roads, looking for telltale signs of IEDs, and hoping that you don't drive over one – it's basically like playing *Minesweeper* in real life. If you find one, you're supposed to radio it in and wait for the nearest Explosive Ordinance Disposal (EOD) team to come dispose of it properly. We hated route clearance for several reasons:

1. EOD teams were spread unbelievably thin and often took hours to get to your location.
2. IEDs were often hidden inside piles of trash, which were nearly ubiquitous in a country that has no organized sanitation removal. Hence, many false alarms.
3. Nothing like driving down the same exact roads at roughly the same time twice per day to make it easy for the enemy to plan attacks.

Because the EOD teams were rarely available, we often had to check out possible IEDs ourselves, in order to avoid being stuck for hours routing traffic a safe distance around what would later turn out to be a totally innocuous garbage heap. Luckily, in the month or so that we were stationed there, we only discovered one IED in Muqdadiyah. This particular IED was "total amateur hour," according to Sergeant First Class Nicholls, upon closer inspection. We happened to be paired up for the mission, and Sergeant Cleary, my gunner, spotted something that looked like a mortar round on the edge of the road as we did our return sweep. After several minutes of anxious examination through our high-powered tank sights, Sergeant First Class Nicholls told me he was going to take a closer look on the ground, so he took another crew member with him and dismounted.

Nicholls gave the device a wide berth, but examined it from several angles, and confirmed: it was indeed a mortar round simply lying in the road, no wires or visible detonation devices. What's more, from the markings on the round, Nicholls suspected it was a smoke round – designed to burn and emit thick smoke to mark or obscure an area, rather than explode and kill people. I'm not sure if the insurgents hoped that we'd drive over it by accident to make it go off, but even if we had, the tank wouldn't have been damaged in the slightest.

"Well, I don't want to pick the damn thing up, even so." I told Nicholls, who had clambered back onto his tank to radio his findings to me.

"Yeah, ditto. But it's going to take EOD hours to get out here, and fuck if I'm sitting out here and missing dinner *again*. I got a better idea."

"Oh shit," I said, but he was already climbing off his tank and out of radio contact before I could reply. He took up a prone firing position behind a dirt mound, aiming his rifle at the mortar round.

There are countless Hollywood movies where the hero shoots his pistol at something stuffed with plastic explosive, and it dutifully explodes in a dazzlingly bright orange cloud of flame. First of all, most explosions aren't bright orange: there generally is very little "flame" involved other than the initial split-second flash, and the rest of it is a grey-brown cloud of debris, which is disappointingly un-photogenic. Second, it's harder to detonate things than one would think: plastic explosive, for instance, can be hit with a hammer, shot with a bullet, even lit on fire, and it's unlikely to explode. Even if you shoot a high explosive tank round into a bunker full of artillery shells, those shells aren't all going to explode, as somebody found out at an abandoned Iraqi ammo depot we later visited. *Most* of them explode, but a significant portion of them just get thrown in every direction by the explosion and lay around the remains of the bunker in an extremely unstable and dangerous state. Don't get me wrong: it's still a shitload of fun to blow things up, it's one of the biggest benefits of going to war. I just didn't have high expectations that Nicholls would have any success with the mortar round we found.

He hit the round with his first shot, it made a loud "pop," and then sizzled for a minute or so, emitting white smoke. And then it was done. I could see Nicholls' grin as he jumped back on his tank and picked up his radio mike.

"Who needs EOD, sir?"

*   *   *

While we were there, the Special Forces "A" team in Muqdadiyah planned a major raid on an insurgent safe-house, and they requested that we put a couple of tanks on standby just in case they bit off a little more than they could chew. We were happy to oblige, so they invited us over to their compound to take part in the planning stages of the raid.

They lived in a walled compound surrounded by barbed wire within the FOB – in the event that the main base was overrun, they could have defended it rather easily. Their motor pool contained a handful of Humvees, a few SUVs for traveling incognito, and some four-wheeler ATVs, each of which had an M240 machine gun mounted on the handlebars, allowing the user to drive and shoot at the same time, or stop and use the ATV as a stable weapons mount. We instantly felt like the cool kids had invited us to sit at their table at lunch.

Inside, we walked through their armory (a bristling collection of sniper rifles and suppressed submachine guns) and into the living room. We were just a few hundred yards from our own barracks area, where we were still living in ramshackle cement buildings without doors or windows, sleeping on cots under mosquito nets, without power or running water. We were showering using water bottles with holes punched in the lids. The Special Forces building was air-conditioned, painted, and well-lit, and the living room held a leather couch with a 60-inch flat-screen TV with a satellite hookup. Each man had his own bedroom, with a real bed and mattress, and they had an indoor shower, laundry machines, and a full kitchen. It was like stepping out of a war zone and into the ultimate bachelor pad, except for the guys cleaning their rifles on the couch. They even had real beer, in defiance of the prohibition on alcohol for U.S. forces in Iraq.

The team commander's mission briefing was short and sweet, in true Green Beret style: they would approach on Humvees, then dismount before they came in audio range of the target house, which he pointed out on the satellite maps their intelligence specialist had downloaded. They expected the house to have several sentries outside, who would be eliminated with silenced pistols to avoid alerting the occupants. They would then clear the house, hustle the insurgents into the Humvees, and roll back. If things went sour, they would "strongpoint" (seize and defend) whatever building was closest and call us in to help deal with the enemy.

The brief completed, we headed back to our own area and prepped our vehicles. We parked our tanks at the main gate as night fell, and settled in to wait things out, tuning our radios to the Special Forces channel. On combat missions, we had been trained to stay in close radio contact with headquarters at all times – even if nothing changed, we would send a radio report every five or ten minutes just to let everyone know we were still out there. In sharp contrast, the Special Forces' radio chatter was both sporadic and informal.

As they pulled out: "Let's go."

Several long minutes later: "Tabasco, this is Big Sexy, turn right ahead."

After another long pause: "Yeah, stop here. Everyone out."

We guessed they were approaching the target house on foot, but we weren't sure. As the minutes dragged on, we thought about trying to raise them on their net just to check in, but there are times when radio silence is critical to a mission, and we didn't want to blow it for them just because we wanted to know what was going on. We didn't hear anything again for 30-40 minutes, and then they suddenly appeared at the gate and rolled inside.

"Hey Bulldawg, thanks for the backup, appreciate it."

Apparently they were done.

*   *   *

Like fighter pilots, tankers place enormous significance on the number of enemy tanks one kills in combat. Now that major combat operations were over in Iraq (at least according to our Commander-in-Chief at the time), there were no more opportunities for us to prove our worth as armored crewmen in a vehicle-to-vehicle duel, however. Or so we thought.

I was lying on my cot one afternoon, trying to catch some sleep after an early morning route clearance mission, when someone ran out of the troop command post and yelled for me. I swore, pulled my flip-flops on, and headed next door, my lack of proper uniform garnering a frown of disapproval from my commander as I walked in.

"What's up, sir?"

"How fast can you be ready to roll out?"

"Ten minutes," I said, turning to leave.

"Stand by, don't get spun up yet."

I shrugged. "Okay. What's going on?"

"White 4 is in contact with a tank."

I was quiet for a second, looking at him closely. "Are you fucking with me, sir?"

He shook his head, and a shiver of excited disbelief ran through me. Twenty minutes previously, a guard post on the perimeter had reported seeing an enemy tank. Lieutenant Pierce and Sergeant First Class Nicholls had been on Quick Reaction Force duty, so they had immediately departed to go check it out, though no one really believed the guard post's report. Anywhere else in Iraq, the guard post would have been laughed at immediately and the report forgotten – it was just too preposterous to be true. In Muqdadiyah, however, two unlikely situations might just have occurred:

1. Insurgents could have snuck inside the wire and stolen an Iraqi Army tank from the thousands that littered the FOB's abandoned motor pool
2. Situated as we were near the eastern edge of Iraq, the Iranians could have crossed the border in force

I was extremely skeptical of either scenario – even Iraqi insurgents trained how to operate one would have to be pretty brain-dead to try to man a single tank against U.S. forces: they would become the biggest and shortest-lived target in history. The second scenario was less ridiculous given the historical tension between the two countries (not to mention Iran's beef with the U.S.), but it was still pretty unlikely that an armored Iranian unit could have crossed into Iraq without anyone noticing. So no one had given the guard post report much credence...until Sergeant First Class Nicholls arrived to check it out and reported making contact with the enemy tank.

This caused all kinds of uproar which we didn't even know about for days. First, Nicholls reported it in to the FOB's command center. One of their "high priority" reporting criteria, based on the off chance that the Iranians might invade, happened to be contact with an armored vehicle, so they immediately passed this information on up the chain to Brigade headquarters, who likewise sent it to 1st Infantry Division headquarters, who then called it in to Multi-National Headquarters in Baghdad. Pretty soon, a General with many stars on his uniform was calling the FOB's operation center wanting to know the size and composition of the Iranian invasion force.

Nicholls had made contact with a tank, alright – an ancient rusted Russian hulk which obviously had been used for target practice many times by the Iraqi tank unit that had been stationed at the base before we invaded. His exact report to the command center was:

"Ramrod X-Ray, Bulldawg White 4. I have identified the tank. It is a T-54/55 with more holes in it than my underwear."

Apparently failing to pick up on the sarcasm about the holes, the command post became fixated on the "T-54/55" part of Nicholls' transmission. Nicholls was implying that he wasn't sure the specific type, whether it was a Soviet T-54 or T-55, which are nearly indistinguishable, especially after being shot at for years. Somehow, the command post missed that nuance, and came to believe that there were *two* tanks: a T-54 *and* a T-55. Apparently delirious at the prospect of reporting on the most significant combat action of the post-invasion period, they ordered him to engage the enemy tanks. So Nicholls clarified his earlier report, clearly stating that this tank – emphasis on tank, *singular* – was no threat at all.

Again, they failed to understand him, or did not believe him, perhaps recalling the report from the guard post that had started the whole fiasco (we never did figure out what the hell they had seen, but it wasn't a tank). Nicholls lost patience at this point, and for shits and giggles, happily complied with the order to fire – tankers don't ever refuse to blow things up, even when it's redundant. Not to be outdone, Brian Pierce took this opportunity to put a second round in the target for good measure. Eventually, the command center staff calmed down a bit, the truth of the matter was sorted out and disseminated to all parties involved, and the tankers were recalled to the FOB. Nicholls got a "kill," Bulldawg Troop got mentioned in some four star general's daily update briefing, and thankfully, World War Three was narrowly averted.

*   *   *

It was at FOB Normandy that I got my first taste of what it was like to be targeted by an IED. In addition to running route clearance missions, we often used the tanks to augment security for logistics convoys moving out of the FOB, providing armored support while the cargo trucks moved through the danger areas in town. On one of these missions, we had interspersed our tanks with the cargo vehicles and were passing the southern edge of Muqdadiyah when a massive *BOOM* rocked the convoy behind me.

I had felt the IED as much as seen it, the shock wave smacking me in the back like a strong shove, even from several hundred meters away. I turned immediately and saw a cloud of dirt-brown smoke rising from the side of the road, with debris raining down on the trucks behind me.

Nicholls, who was at the front of the column, beat me to the radio report, calling in the contact quickly but calmly. I keyed the radio to the rest of the patrol, asking for a damage report to see if anyone was injured, and to see why the trucks in the "kill zone" had stopped moving. A Humvee commander close to the truck that had been hit jumped out and climbed the side of the truck, yelling at the crew. They were okay, and the truck appeared undamaged, but it had stalled from the blast. It started when they tried it, however, and I gave the order to move again and clear out of the area, lest the insurgents follow up with a small-arms attack on our stationary convoy. Had it been a patrol of tanks alone, we might have stuck around to try to deal with the enemy, but our mission was to get these vehicles safely on their way, and that took priority.

Once the convoy was past the town, Nicholls and I turned around and returned to the scene of the attack, approaching extremely cautiously and scanning the roadside closely to ensure there wasn't a second IED. We saw nothing to indicate a second attack, and soon found three gaping holes about ten feet apart in the tarmac – it had been a daisy-chained IED, no less. While I secured the road and blocked traffic, Nicholls inspected the site more closely on the ground, finding the detonation wires, which led back to an abandoned mud hut about 50 meters from the road. The hut had a perfect view of the road and a thickly overgrown field at its back, through which our assailants had escaped after the attack. Even if we had been quick enough to realize where the bombs had been detonated from right after the attack, the insurgents had disappeared into the field before we could have done much about it.

The hut showed signs of men having lived there for several days – food scraps, the remains of a fire, and feces. Knowing the logistics convoy operated on a regular basis, the men had laid their trap and then waited for their moment. They had even set up two short stakes in the field in front of the house as crude aiming devices: from the hut, the stakes lined up with the edges of the kill zone. It was a patient, well-planned operation. Nicholls and I agreed that the buildings could be used again in the exact same manner and needed to be demolished. He was worried, however, that the 2-2 Infantry command center would be reticent about firing main gun rounds at a house, abandoned or not.

"Let's just shoot it," he said. "Better to ask forgiveness than permission, right?"

SGT Cleary and I swiveled our turret, and put a high explosive round into the building, crumbling a wall. The 2-2 Infantry command center was on the radio immediately, demanding to know what the hell was going on. Nicholls told them we were demolishing a building [pause for round two – *BOOM!*] used for ambushes. They were miffed we hadn't cleared it with them first, but let it go. We finished off the building, toppling the remaining walls by ramming them with the front of our tanks, and then headed back to base.

*   *   *

While we were in Muqdadiyah, our normal Troop Executive Officer, First Lieutenant O'Brien, was detached to another unit, lending them the firepower of his Bradley and a couple of our tanks. During this time, Joey Thomas, our troop Fire Support Officer, served as the substitute troop Executive Officer, which he handled admirably. The Executive Officer is technically second-in-command of the troop, but his real job is making sure all of the vehicles are properly maintained. That's a tough job, especially in Iraq, where the physical conditions and unrelenting pace of operations take an enormous toll on the vehicles. As an added bonus, our habit of hopping from base to base every few weeks as the Division's mobile reserve meant that the spare parts we ordered never caught up to us – they were constantly arriving a few weeks after we left each base, and naturally getting put to use by the units we had left behind.

The American soldier is known for being resourceful and innovative, which is generally true, but is also a euphemism for being good at breaking the rules when necessary. Every unit has individuals who are even more resourceful than most, and we were no exception. Sergeant First Class Peterson was leading fuel convoy escorts later during our tour when one of his Humvees blew a tire. As usual given our supply woes, he was totally out of spares. He happened to be near a major support FOB at the time, and after a brief search at the supply depot (who wouldn't resupply him because all of their tires were ear-marked for other units already), he found a motor pool with four or five Humvees in pristine condition, each of which carried a spare. Given how clean they were, the Humvees were clearly not used for missions outside the FOB – they were glorified golf carts that got washed weekly and never left the wire. Peterson and his men were in the midst of stealing two of the spares when a Sergeant from the unit that owned the tires strolled into the motor pool.

"Woah, what are you guys doing?"

Peterson had to think fast. "Hm? Oh, I talked to your NCO inside and he said to take them."

"Sergeant First Class Johnson?"

Peterson smiled. "That's the guy."

"Oh, okay," the soldier said. "Lemme give you a hand."

Charlie Troop was similarly short on spare tires on another occasion, so they found a massive pile of them at their nearest support FOB. Their Executive Officer, Dan Cho, argued for a while with the depot personnel, begging and pleading to get even a few of them released, to no avail – they were all reserved for other units who hadn't shown up to get them yet. Being a resourceful, adaptive individual, he thanked them and left. Then he took his cargo truck to the opposite side of the depot, well out of sight of the depot offices, sent two scouts scrambling over the fence, and used his cargo truck's crane to hoist the spare tires over the fence.

We reached a critical point in Muqdadiyah where almost all of our vehicles were broken and still no parts were coming in. As interim Executive Officer, Joey had tried for several weeks to get our parts sent on to us, with no luck. The system having failed, he grabbed some soldiers and ran a logistical convoy back to the nearest support FOB, which had a large parts depot. Knowing he was going to get stonewalled from the start without the proper paperwork, he just sauntered into the depot and started loading the stuff we needed onto his truck. When you look like you know what you're doing in the Army, you can get away with a lot. About halfway through his spree, however, a warrant officer who knew better caught sight of them and accosted Joey.

"What's going on here, sir?"

There was no sense bullshitting him, so Joey handed him the list of parts he needed and truthfully told him we were about to be combat ineffective if we didn't get them. The warrant officer flipped through a couple pages worth of notes.

"Woah...this is a couple million dollars' worth of parts here, sir."

Joey laughed, "I know!"

If he had been an asshole, the guy could have gotten Joey in some serious hot water at that point.

"Well, fuck...let's see what we can do for you, sir."

It's hit or miss with supply guys – sometimes you get everything you need and more, other times, nothing.

CHAPTER FIVE

"Bulldawg X-Ray, Red 1: negative enemy contact, continuing to conduct checkpoint operations. Current ambient air temperature is 117 degrees, current take in enemy weapons, vehicles, contraband, and personnel – zero."
-Lieutenant Vince Taylor

May rolled around, and with it, orders to report to FOB Summerall, a post manned by a battalion of artillerymen outside of Baiji, a small city north of Tikrit. They were delighted to see us, but they had nowhere to put us, so we camped out in their newly built basketball gym for a few weeks. They soon procured several large canvas tents for our use – but we would have to build the wooden floors for them, because they couldn't scrape together enough Iraqi contractors to do so. They did hire a few local carpenters to help out, with whom Staff Sergeant Peiper quickly bonded, trying to teach them some useful English phrases. He started them easy, with simple, one-word profanities, before moving on to some more complex ones. They loved every minute of it.

"…okay, okay, good. Now try this one: 'Dip my balls in milk and put me in a room full of kittens.'"

"What this mean?" The Iraqi asked, innocently.

Peiper scratched his head, and decided charades was the best way to proceed.

"Okay: 'dip my balls,' like this…"

Army NCOs are famous for their extensively vulgar vocabulary –

with great justification – and it rubs off on everyone else quickly. When I went back home for R&R leave months later, I found I had to work hard to tone down my own language, it had become so much a part of my everyday vernacular. I dropped a noticeable F-bomb in the middle of a polite dinner conversation at my fiancée's house, which pretty much silenced everyone.

"Sorry," I said. "I'm probably going to be doing that a lot."

Luckily, they had a good sense of humor about it. But my language skills paled in comparison to the NCOs. Peiper liked to say that certain activities were: "more fun than kicking over blind people's walking sticks." One of Nicholls' favorite phrases went like this:

"What's up, Sergeant First Class Nicholls?"

"Dicks and choppers, sir – which are you going down on?"

Nicknames are fairly common throughout units, too – before we left Schweinfurt, the older officers dubbed me "The Kid," being both the junior officer in the troop, and appearing younger than my 23 years as well. The older NCOs used to love asking me: "Does your mommy know you're playing Army today?" It stuck, to a certain degree, and Sergeant Cleary painted it onto the back of my tank hatch along with the *Playboy* bunny logo (for no reason other than that he wanted to get our picture in the magazine, but that never panned out). Vince Taylor earned the nickname "Frodo" for being short, and Brian Pierce got the unfortunate title "Mongo," after the dim-witted strong guy in *Blazing Saddles*. Later, Staff Sergeant Barnes would give me a new nickname: "Dex," after the title character in the cartoon *Dexter's Laboratory*, a dig at my habit of using SAT words and generally being a nerd. We learned to put ego aside and embrace the names.

The soldiers had it far worse, however. Between Peiper and Kean, our platoon members had been christened with the following nicknames: Bitchass, Shithead, Cum-dumpster, Dickhole, and Butt-stain. They used these often enough that people actually knew who they were referring to:

"Hey, Steve, where's Dickhole?"

"Uh, I think he went to get some chow with Shithead, Sergeant."

*　　　*　　　*

At FOB Summerall, our primary mission – as it had been throughout Iraq so far – was to secure the routes leading to and from the FOB. The Army's overall objective in Iraq was still to train the nascent Iraqi Army, but Bulldawg Troop rarely collaborated with them on missions, even after the Iraqi government took over authority in June. For those of us stuck in the drudgery of daily route clearance missions, it felt frustratingly like treading water, just waiting for our time in country to be up. My section of tanks would often spend the night parked a mile or so off one of the main roads, overwatching the road in an attempt to catch insurgents in the act of placing IEDs. One or two of us on each tank would be alert and watching our assigned areas, usually for an hour at a time, while the others rested. The first fifteen minutes of guard duty go quickly – you're still adjusting to the dark, identifying shadows and planning responses to different scenarios in your mind. Then time stands still. You check your watch and wait. A car passes, a dog barks. You wait some more. You send in a radio report, and then you wait. You stand up and stretch, you take a leak off the side of the tank, you take another peek through the thermal sights, and then you check your watch...and just three minutes have passed. And in an hour or two, you'll be back on watch, doing it all again.

On one night, while Sergeant Cleary napped down in his gunner's seat, I took up my customary position seated atop our ice chest on the turret, and scanned the road for several minutes. Seeing nothing, I decided to cool off a bottle of water in the ice, knowing I would want it later. I usually kept one tucked inside the tank at my station. In the dark, I groped for it, leaning down through my hatch. It was half-empty, but I'm not one to waste unnecessarily, so I stuffed it in the ice and let it chill for a half hour or so. When I judged it had cooled enough, I pulled it out and took a long, swig, chugging thirstily. About two seconds into drinking, I thought I smelled cigarette smoke, and figured that Cleary must have woken up for a smoke. I stopped drinking, however, when I realized I hadn't smelled smoke, but *tasted* it. Cleary had found my bottle earlier, mistaken it for trash, and used it to dispose of a couple butts he had smoked. I had some harsh words for him after that, but I had to laugh with him, after I gargled a few sodas and got some of the awful taste out of my mouth.

*   *   *

FOB Summerall was a *big* post, and it was a hefty 15-minute walk from our tents over to the chow hall for breakfast or dinner. In the midsummer Iraqi heat, wearing 30 plus pounds of gear, this simple stroll turned into a panting, sweat-soaked ordeal, so that many guys chose to eat MREs or forgo a meal altogether, rather than make the trek for some mediocre Army food. The scout platoons had Humvees and could shuttle their guys back and forth fairly easily, but for the tank platoons without Humvees, making the trip by tank was more trouble than it was worth. There were several other Humvees floating around the troop, however, in particular the Executive Officer's Humvee, which First Lieutenant O'Brien used to drive to and from the FOB headquarters building when he was needed there for meetings or to be given orders.

He let us borrow it a few times, but after he was summoned by headquarters one evening only to find his Humvee had been "borrowed" without his permission for a chow run, his patience ran out and he locked the wheel with a chain and padlock. It was a legitimate move, but he was also somewhat patronizing about the whole affair, so naturally we took exception. Staff Sergeant Peiper had an urgent mission to pick up spare parts from another area of the post one afternoon, and succeeded in obtaining O'Brien's permission to use his Humvee one last time.

"Just so long as it's not for a chow run, and you'll be right back."

"Yes, sir – no chow."

Peiper made his trip, and also took that opportunity to switch the padlock with another identical one, for which he had two sets of keys. He dutifully handed one key to First Lieutenant O'Brien when he got back to our motor pool, locking the wheel as ordered. And for the next several nights, after O'Brien had gone to sleep, Peiper would send someone in our platoon out to the motor pool to unlock the Humvee and park it someplace else. O'Brien, who was dead certain he had the only key for the lock, would come out in the morning to find his Humvee parked drunkenly, out of alignment with the rest of the neatly parked trucks, or parked behind the showers, or at the very far end of our large motor pool. He was pretty pissed, but was smart enough not to let us see it, partly because he had no idea who had done it or how they had pulled it off.

*   *   *

One day a route clearance mission took us out past the Baiji oil refinery, which was the terminus for a large pipeline coming in from the northeast of the country. The pipeline itself crossed the Tigris underwater, and the crossing point now featured a small civilian FOB, home to the contractors working on rebuilding the underwater pipeline. Apparently, at some point during the initial invasion, some crafty bastard in the air operations targeting team had correctly guessed that if we bombed the bridge that ran across the river at the same point, the falling debris would cut the underwater pipeline as well, and now our tax dollars were hard at work rebuilding that same pipe. We discovered that the civilians' FOB had an excellent chow hall which happily served soldiers, so Peiper and I rearranged the mission schedule a bit so that we were coincidentally right by the FOB around lunchtime.

We pulled up to the gate, which was guarded by several Kurdish soldiers. Unsure of the entry procedures, Peiper pulled off his helmet in order to talk to the closest Kurd, who sauntered over, smiling.

"Hey, you got somewhere in here we can park?"

The guard smiled and nodded, clearly not understanding a word of what Peiper had said.

"Okay, is the whorehouse up there, too?"

Nodding.

"With all the chicks? The ones we can fuck?"

More smiles and nods.

"Okay, 'cause I want to go fuck some chicks, man. Rock on, thanks, man."

Lunch was excellent, and well worth the trip. The closest we had come to fresh fruit in months was apple sauce or canned peaches, but they had a huge bowl of fresh fruit on ice, which we helped ourselves to liberally. Peiper was a big fan of kiwis, and grabbed one for our newest soldier, a Private named Jeffries who had recently joined our platoon. He was a quiet, unassuming kid, fresh out of basic training and still used to treating his superiors with a fearful respect bordering on awe. Peiper and Kean had taken him under their collective wing to make sure he was "raised" with the proper 4th Platoon spirit instilled in him.

"Eat your kiwi, Jeffries," Peiper ordered.

"Yes, Sergeant." Jeffries picked up the kiwi and started peeling it.

"You know why we eat kiwis, right, Jeffries?"

"Yes, Sergeant."

"Why's that, Jeffries?"

"Because they make your dick grow, Sergeant."

"Fuckin' A, Jeffries. And I've seen your dick, dude: you could use some help."

Over lunch, we chatted with a few of the contractors, who explained the work they were doing on the pipeline. Several months after we left Baiji, some insurgents with a keen sense of humor waited until the contractors completely fixed the underwater pipeline, and then blew the bridge up again, dropping tons of concrete into the water and cutting the line once more.

They targeted the pipeline aboveground while we were in Baiji, too. Two or three paid Iraqi security guards lived in small tents at regular intervals along the entire pipeline, basically just sitting there all day and night, and watching their few yards of pipeline. The tents were located several miles apart, however, and definitely not within sight of each other, so they were largely ineffective. One night while we were back at FOB Summerall, one of our troopers rushed into our tent, grabbing his video camera and pausing to shout, "The pipeline's been hit!" as he ran back outside.

We dutifully piled out to rubberneck, and sure enough, several miles away there was an enormous geyser of flame erupting on the horizon. It was bright enough to read the paper by, even at that distance. The insurgents had simply walked up to the pipe, strapped some explosives to it, and detonated them, cutting the pipeline and setting the gushing oil aflame. The only way they could put it out was by stopping the flow entirely, but miles of oil were still in the system, and it burned for quite a while. Not that the local firefighters would have been much help, had they tried to put it out themselves: I've got an utterly priceless photograph of the Baiji fire station, showing three brand new fire engines all parked in their garage...*facing in*. To respond to an emergency, they would have had to slowly back each one out.

CHAPTER SIX

"It's hotter than two rats fucking in a wool sock."
-Staff Sergeant Kean

In August, we received fantastic news: a civilian-run dining hall at FOB Summerall would be opening soon. Army-run chow halls all have the same cooking process: take previously prepared meals that have been frozen in plastic bags, heat them in boiling water, cut open the bags, and serve. When they got fresh food (rarely), it was generally limited to a few bananas or a side salad, and there were only about ten different meals available, which got old fast. So we were pretty stoked that the civilians were opening up: that meant fresh, hot meals, prepared from scratch four times a day (breakfast, lunch, dinner, and "midnight chow" for folks with night operations), with a wide variety of options at each meal, and even ridiculous luxuries like Surf-and-Turf Night and make-your-own ice cream sundae stations. The new chow hall was open for exactly one week before we received our orders to head back to 1-4 CAV headquarters at FOB Mackenzie. Where our Army-run chow hall was waiting for us.

When I first took command of my platoon back in Germany, I learned two things immediately from Vince Taylor, the outgoing platoon leader. First, I was lucky enough to have two of the best section sergeants in the squadron in Staff Sergeants Kean and Peiper, whose strengths complemented each other perfectly. Unfortunately, I was also getting the squadron's worst platoon sergeant in the form of Sergeant First Class Gilman, whose slovenly appearance and lack of leadership instincts earned him the nickname of "Dude," after the protagonist in *Big Lebowski*. The name fit him to a tee.

"Dude" had been fired in his first attempt at being a platoon sergeant, for numerous displays of incompetence that culminated in his refusal to take his crew out for gunnery training one night, claiming their lack of sleep would make it too dangerous to do the training. I guess he expected every combat mission to be preceded by a good night's rest, too. He was now being given a second shot, following the Army's ironclad logic that a guy who had failed miserably in training should be given more responsibility – for instance, a platoon heading into combat. He had been mostly napping his way through Iraq, but he hadn't fucked up badly enough that I could try firing him again.

I later learned from his crew that Dude would often force his gunner out of the turret to help him command the tank, since he was incapable of giving his driver clear commands when maneuvering the tank. Staff Sergeant Kean – his subordinate – basically commanded their section while they were out on mission together, so Dude was essentially a fifth wheel in the platoon: a lousy tank commander that everyone else had to pick up the slack for. His duties boiled down to attending meetings with the First Sergeant when back at base, and passing that info down to Kean and Peiper to execute, which they usually had to double-check for accuracy because Dude was notoriously bad at taking notes. Nine times out of ten, after Dude and I came out of a meeting together, Peiper and Kean would have to find me after Dude had given them his guidance, and I would have to explain what had really happened at the meeting, and what their tasks were. Most of our interactions back at base consisted of him complaining to me about how tough the platoon had it, and me reminding him that I wasn't going to go bitch to the commander without a recommendation for how to fix it.

Over the course of two months that summer, Dude managed to leave his rifle under the gun tube *twice*, so that when his gunner elevated the gun, Dude's rifle was crushed, *twice*. Once is an embarrassing oversight, twice in as many months is inexcusable. Whenever we were out on missions, if I gave Dude a grid (the series of numbers we used to indicate a position on a map), I invariably needed to repeat it two or three times. He became annoyed with me for making him repeat back to me every grid I sent him, but it was the only way I could ensure he got it right. One time he even got lost on the way to our observation posts north of Samarra – an area where we had been conducting missions for *months,* static positions where we parked our tanks and sat for days on end, which hadn't changed once in those long months. Somehow, Dude couldn't find them.

He was terrible at radio reporting, one of his primary duties – the man seemed incapable of talking on the radio and doing anything else at the same time. Often, one of his crew members, impatient that he was ignoring the radio, would respond for him while he was trying to guide his driver, but usually, I would cut them off and demand to speak with Dude himself. I wasn't going to allow him to continue his bad habits, as much as I could help it.

As Dude's wingman, Staff Sergeant Kean should have been given an extra medal for having to deal with Dude on the most frequent basis. To his immense credit, he managed to largely conceal his lack of respect for Dude from the soldiers, dutifully maintaining the chain of command as much as possible. Sometimes, however, Dude sorely tried Kean's professionalism in this regard. As much as we could, while in Iraq we avoided driving through fields that were clearly being farmed, in order to maintain good relations with the local farmers. It was an unwritten, standing rule – if you could avoid damaging anything valuable to an Iraqi, you did. Dude missed this memo, apparently, because one day he blithely parked his tank in the middle of a freshly-plowed field, destroying the neat rows the farmer had so recently labored to complete.

Kean later told me that he completely lost it, had Dude meet him behind the tanks, where the soldiers couldn't hear them, and then laid into Gilman like he was the lowliest Private in the Army. Any other platoon sergeant would never have tolerated this treatment from a subordinate, but Dude just stood there, nodding sheepishly. This lack of backbone disgusted Kean even more, but all he could do was walk away, find the farmer, and give him a case of MREs and some water bottles to try to make it up to him.

One night, Dude and Kean were pulling observation post duties north of Samarra. It was a particularly clear night, and Kean and crew were admiring the night sky when a large, bright shooting star raced across the sky, from one edge of the horizon to the other. The radio crackled to life.

"Bulldawg X-Ray, Green 4!"

Staff Sergeant Kean groaned – Dude sounded excited on the radio, which was never a good sign. X-Ray responded.

"Green 4, this is X-Ray."

"Roger, enemy contact! One rocket, grid MC 192 754, unable to determine the point-of-origin, over!"

"Roger Green 4, we acknowledge you are taking incoming rocket fire at your location, can you estimate size of round and general direction it came from, over?"

"Uh, it didn't impact at my location, it passed overhead…stand by for direction, over."

Staff Sergeant Kean decided it was time to put an end to things before they got any more ridiculous, so he picked up his own hand-mike, trying to conceal his disgust.

"X-Ray, Green 3."

"Green 3, X-Ray – did you get a good look at that rocket Green 4 saw? You guys are in visual range of each other, right?"

"Yeah, X-Ray, I saw it – that wasn't a rocket, it was a shooting star, over."

Dude, indignant, was sure he had seen a rocket, and despite his own crew trying to explain it to him, and then Kean trying to explain it to him over the radio, he could not be convinced otherwise.

"No, man – it had a white trail after it. Stars don't do that!"

To this day, Dude believes it was a rocket. He was already the butt of many jokes among the troop's officers and senior NCOs by that point, but the "rocket" episode made him infamous throughout the entire troop.

*   *   *

1-4 CAV needed our help back at FOB Mackenzie because our logistics convoys were getting hammered by IEDs and complex ambushes as they passed north of Samarra. As at our previous locations, our mission was to secure that route, but because FOB Mackenzie was a solid 45 minutes from Samarra, we based operations out of a tiny outpost close to Samarra that housed a communications link between Squadron's two bases, known as the retrans site (for "retransmission").

The retrans site was a real dump. We'd been in some crappy

locations before, but this one immediately set a new low. It was on the edge of a road within sight of Samarra, and featured a short, dusty mound which supported the radio antennas. The mound had a small area of flat sand about the size of a basketball court at its base, which was surrounded by a low earthen wall, reinforced haphazardly with some razor wire. It was poorly fortified and horribly exposed – the only shelter was a tarp awkwardly covering a hole scraped out of the mound, where the lone commo soldier sat and monitored the radios all day and night. There was no generator for electricity, no place to sit in the shade (save for the dark green tarp, which heated up like a sauna during the day), a single plywood outhouse, and a mangy dog who begged for MRE scraps and who we imaginatively named Rex. Save for short trips back to FOB Mackenzie to shower and eat some hot chow, this would be our home for the foreseeable future.

Along with our sister tank platoon, we worked out a rotation system that would barely cover manning the Samarra observation posts and guarding the retrans site. Two tanks would occupy the observation posts along the road outside Samarra for eight hours, then go back to the retrans site for eight hours (switching out with another pair of tanks), and continue switching for 48 hours straight. The crews would then spend 48 hours manning the guard positions at the retrans site, swapping out on 8 hour shifts. Our time off consisted of a 48-hour recovery period, which included travel time to and from the retrans site, and by necessity it was mainly spent doing maintenance on the tanks, and possibly, showering and sleeping for a few hours. Soon enough, however, with vehicles breaking and soldiers going on R&R, it became impossible to rotate anyone back, and we had crews staying at the site for a week or more, spending 12 hours on their tank, then 12 hours off at the retrans site, repeating several times, then working eight-hour guard shifts at the site for a day or so before maybe sneaking back to Mackenzie for a brief 24 hours. It wore us all down fast, and the excruciating August heat didn't help.

Rex the dog became such a ubiquitous part of the life at the retrans site that the outpost was soon renamed FOB Rex. Rex was a mangy mutt you could smell from a mile away, but we loved him and welcomed any distraction from the day-to-day drudgery of life out there. About a month in, we discovered that Rex was, in fact, female – and she was very much in heat, which caused her to spend most of her time with her head buried in her crotch, licking industriously. I got back from 12-hour observation mission one day and set up my cot in the shade of my tank, hoping to get a little sleep before the sun moved too far and I sweated myself awake again. Exhausted, I passed out, but soon awoke to an odd sensation – Rex, lovingly licking my face. I've never missed the ability to shower so acutely.

*   *   *

1-26 Infantry was technically responsible for securing Samarra, but back in the spring, insurgents had attacked their outpost with a massive car bomb, killing a number of the infantrymen. Without a way to secure that base from further attacks, 1-26 withdrew from the city, only patrolling sporadically. Predictably, insurgents flocked to Samarra in droves, claiming the city for themselves. But one unit remained: a Special Forces "A" Team, a handful of Green Berets in the middle of an insurgent-held city.

Manning our observation posts outside Samarra, we regularly listened in on the 1-26 Infantry net: since they were our neighboring unit, it was good to keep tabs on what they were up to, especially when there was enemy contact in the city. Generally the contact was brief: a few mortar rounds were fired across the river at their FOB, or someone emptied an AK-47 clip at a Humvee patrol, using the ever-popular insurgent "spray and pray" technique: (1) hold the weapon out at arms' length around the corner of a building, (2) pull the trigger, (3) run. On one night, however, we heard several loud explosions, and then heavy small arms fire. The Green Berets' safe house was under attack.

The fight was going strong after 30 minutes, tracers still ricocheting up into the night sky, punctuated by the occasional muffled thump of a grenade detonating. We heard the radio crackle to life; the Special Forces team was calling 1-26 Infantry, and given the prolonged fight, my guess was that they were going to ask for some reinforcements.

"Spader X-Ray, this is ODA 621, over." I could hear heavy gunfire in the background, but somehow, the special operator managed to sound bored.

"Go ahead, 621."

"Roger, we've been in contact for a while here, any chance you guys could put together an ammo resupply for us? We're getting a little low."

I had to laugh: I'm sure the infantrymen were chomping at the bit to join the fight, but the Special Forces guys had it well under control.

"This is Spader X-Ray, roger – what do you need?"

"Appreciate it. We need...uhh, where's that list? 10,000 rounds of 5.56mm, another 10,000 linked 7.62mm...hold on."

We heard a machine gun firing a sustained burst, then the Green Beret picked up his radio microphone again.

"...sorry about that. A case of fragmentation grenades, and any M240 rounds you can scrounge up would be great."

*   *   *

By late summer, 1st Infantry Division had decided to begin operations to retake Samarra, but intelligence estimates varied wildly on the number of insurgents that had taken up residence there. The analysts were sure that at least 300 hardcore Saddam loyalists controlled the city, with up to a thousand foreign fighters augmenting them, all spoiling for a fight. To gain a better understanding of what clearing the city would be like, 2nd Brigade and 1-4 CAV launched a series of night-time raids on the perimeter of the city, called Operation Cajun Mousetrap (the Army picks operation names at random to avoid hinting at the intent of the mission). We continued to maintain our observation posts during these missions, and though I was back at FOB Mackenzie when the first raid was launched, I had front row seats to Cajun Mousetrap 2 several days later. Though Bulldawg Troop would not be participating in the raid, our Troop Commander (Captain Hoffman) and Executive Officer (First Lieutenant O'Brien) brought their vehicles out from Mackenzie to set up a troop command post overwatching the city. They had nothing to command from their command post, they just wanted to watch the action, too.

And it was quite a show. The operation started on the far side of the city, with 1-26 Infantry moving onto a bridge across the Tigris to clear it of road blocks and enemy positions. They encountered resistance immediately, and after destroying barricades and machine gun nests with Bradley and tank fire, they called in Apache support, who lit up the area with 30mm chain gun and rocket fire. The Apaches soon became locked in a bitter firefight with a large group of insurgents occupying an abandoned Iraqi Police station, and once they had received clearance to do so, the Air Force dropped a 500-pound bomb on the building.

As soon as we heard the report over the net that an airstrike was inbound, we had the cameras out and ready. It was spectacular, exactly like the "shock and awe" explosions we had seen in Baghdad on TV, except that we felt the shockwave even from two miles away. A massive fireball lit up the night sky, and flaming debris and shrapnel arced out of the blast site and over the rooftops. There was a certain amount of not-so-professional cheering and whooping over the net, and then we settled back down to watch some more. I felt like making some popcorn.

Next up, 1-77 Armor and 1-18 Infantry approached the city from the north along Route Grape, driving past our positions as they looked for the road they would use to enter the city. Their mission was a simple "movement to contact," which is Army-speak for "keep driving until you find someone to shoot at." They were to enter Samarra, drive in a big loop through several blocks, destroy any insurgents encountered, and then leave. Except that they missed their turn in the dark, and we watched as their long column of armored vehicles drove past the entrance road and continued away from the city. They stopped soon after, idling in a disorganized jumble on the road in obvious confusion.

Grinning, I flipped my radio switch to talk to Peiper: "Hey, Green 2: you seeing this?"

"Yeah, roger. How are they fucking *lost?*"

I laughed. "Think I should go down there and help out a little? 'Hey, see the lights and buildings, that way? That's Samarra. You want to go that way.'"

"Those guys could fuck up a wet dream."

They soon figured it out, and after a laborious U-turn process, entered the city as planned. They were doing fine, trading machine gun fire sporadically with insurgents, until a tank "threw track" in the city, the road wheels coming out of the massive loop of treads on one side of the tank, disabling it immediately. It's about the worst thing that can happen to a tank in combat – there's no quick and easy fix. Either you spend an hour or so opening the loop of track, dragging it back into place, carefully walking the tank wheels back onto the treads, and then closing the loop again, or you leave the track and tow the tank as is, destroying the exposed road wheels in the process. As they were actively battling insurgents, they wisely chose to just tow the tank out of there. Though they were several blocks in, we were able to track their progress by the running firefight, tracers ricocheting over the rooftops and explosions backlighting the buildings. It turned ugly when the insurgents began firing rocket-propelled grenades, the white flashes of exploding warheads lighting the city blocks like flashbulbs. 2nd Brigade responded with two 500-pound bombs this time, which immediately knocked out all power to the city, shrouding it in darkness.

Meanwhile, Anvil Troop had begun its raid on the southeastern quadrant of the city. Unlike the 2nd Brigade elements, Anvil Troop had actionable intelligence in their sector, and planned to conduct a snatch-and-grab raid on a building thought to contain high value targets. As they entered the city, however, they encountered several groups of insurgents busily digging up weapons caches, hurriedly pulling rifles and rocket-propelled grenade launchers out of holes in the ground. Anvil engaged them immediately, with help from Darkhorse Troop in their Kiowa helicopters. Under the sustained fire, the enemy quickly retreated to a large building, which jumped to the top of the airstrike priority list.

Along the eastern edge of the city, our Red Platoon Bradleys had established a series of positions to prevent any enemy forces from escaping during the raids. Red 2's gunner, Sergeant Newsome, was monitoring the Anvil Troop net and relaying the highlights to us on the Bulldawg Troop net.

"The insurgents have all holed up in one building," he reported.

"Fuck yeah!" My gunner, Sergeant Cleary, grinned at me.

Newsome came back over the net. "They're going to drop a 2,000 pound bomb. Stand by…"

"…impact in 20 seconds."

Across the battlefield, crewmembers were hastily awakened for the show.

"…ten seconds."

Cameras up, breath held.

"…impact."

Nothing. We waited until Newsome came back on the net.

"Yeah, they're saying that it was a dud."

There were sustained boos and catcalls across the net, followed by colorful descriptions of the depth of incompetence found only among fighter pilots.

"Hold on…okay, they're going to drop another right on top of it."

According to the Anvil Troopers close to the scene, the combined 4,000 pounds of high explosive utterly demolished the building. A massive column of cement-grey dust rose from the area, and the noise of the blast echoed over the city. As Anvil continued into the city, they encountered more resistance, but this time, the insurgents were clustered in a large crowd in the street, firing at the troopers from behind a low wall. 2nd Brigade detached another fighter from the stack overhead, which swooped into position with a 500-pound bomb, ready to rock. Newsome continued the play-by-play for our benefit.

"Nope, they're canceling that 500-pounder mission. A drone orbiting the area just identified women and children in the street nearby."

Sergeant First Class Nicholls, disappointed, chimed in with his two cents: "Fuck 'em! Wrong place, wrong time. Besides, women and children are just insurgent-factories and insurgents-in-training."

Faced with inflicting civilian casualties, Anvil withdrew without raiding their target. Across the city, 1-26 Infantry, 1-77 Armor, and 1-18 Infantry also pulled out of the city, their objectives accomplished, with no casualties among U.S. forces but a heavy toll – as usual, precise counts were impossible – exacted on the insurgents in the city. As dawn broke, we watched 1-77 Armor leave Samarra, hauling their broken tank with them. The tank's exposed road wheels were completely aflame, rings of fire spinning in the half-light, leaving a 50-yard trail of burning rubber in their wake just like the Delorean in *Back to the Future*. It may have been a less-than-dignified exit for U.S. forces, but the scorecard was clearly in our favor.

As the large-scale mission wound down, the Bulldawg elements that had come out from FOB Mackenzie to watch the battle began to regroup and prepare to return to base. I yawned – it had been a long night. First Lieutenant O'Brien, in his Bradley, called Captain Hoffman on his tank to see if he was ready to lead the convoy back in.

"Bulldawg 6, Bulldawg 5, over." He waited several seconds.

"Bulldawg 6, this is Bulldawg 5." Another wait. "Bulldawg 6, Bulldawg 5."

By now, all of the troop had noted the absence of a response. As O'Brien continued to try to establish radio contact, we turned up the volume to hear how this latest comedy would pan out.

O'Brien was getting frustrated: "…Any crewmember on Bulldawg 6, this is Bulldawg 5, over!"

I decided to fan the flames a bit, and whispered into my hand-mike: "Shhh…somebody's sleeping!"

Captain Hoffman had taken a nap, and whichever crewmember he had left on watch had also fallen asleep, which would earn him a scathing reprimand when they all awoke. It took O'Brien driving up to Hoffman's tank to wake them up. It was an embarrassing moment for Hoffman, to say the least – his entire crew had fallen asleep in enemy territory.

*   *   *

Somehow, after our tanks had driven the route often enough, there formed a small mound outside the perimeter of FOB Rex which was about three feet high. It was a fun little bump to ride over in the tank, enough to rock the tank's heavy suspension and elicit a "Whoo!" from any passengers. Staff Sergeant Peiper soon got it into his head that he was going to try to jump his tank off this bump, and after I'd had a chance to set up my video camera, he hit it at full speed one afternoon, and actually managed to get the entire 70-ton tank airborne. Unfortunately, the violent landing also broke his .50 cal machine gun mount, but I think the tax-payers would agree that it was worth it for the footage.

One of our priorities along the route north of Samarra was to make it as hard as possible for any IEDs to be hidden along the highway, starting with clearing the undergrowth choking the roadside in some places. Normally this is a task that an engineer unit would handle, but we were low down on the priority list, so we improvised: we escorted a fuel truck along the road, stopping occasionally to pay out the hoses and squirt diesel fuel onto the plants. Diesel fuel, however, is not as easy to light on fire as one might expect.

We tried lighting paper on fire with a lighter and dropping it on the fuel, but the wind blew it out before the fire could catch. Next,

Peiper tossed a smoke grenade, which doesn't explode, but does generate a lot of heat. It got some of the plants to smolder, but still no outright flames. Finally, frustrated, Peiper had a flash of brilliance. I saw him reach for the radio on his tank.

"Hey Green 1 – move back and get your camera out."

I groaned, keying my own microphone. "No gunfire, Green 2."

"Yeah roger, roger," he answered, slightly peeved.

I saw him buttoning up his tank, locking the hatches tight, and realized what he was going to do. The M1 Abrams tank has two smoke grenade launchers mounted on the turret. They fire special smoke and white phosphorus grenades which are designed to launch into the air above the tank and then explode, generating a thick screen of white smoke behind which the tank may displace without being seen by the enemy. It's a spectacular sight, like smoky fireworks close to the ground. As usual, Peiper's brilliance paid off: he launched his smoke screen, the white phosphorus grenades caused the brush to burst into flame, and we got a kick-ass picture out of it.

*   *   *

One morning on our way out to the observation posts, Peiper and I found an IED along the highway just outside of Samarra: a mound of recently-overturned dirt, with a visible wire protruding that looked like it ran all the way back to the nearest buildings on the edge of Samarra. We secured the area, with Peiper blocking one side of the highway and my tank the other, and called for an explosive ordinance disposal (EOD) team. They pulled up about 45 minutes later in a couple of modified Humvees with large storage containers on the backs. I hopped down off my tank and pointed out the IED to their senior NCO.

"Okay, I see it," he told me.

In my experience, normal protocol for EOD at this juncture would have been to go yank the wires out from a safe-ish distance, slap together a couple of blocks of C-4 (plastic explosive), have one guy walk up to the bomb (praying that the bomb could only have been detonated by the wires they just removed, and that there wasn't a backup wireless device), carefully put the C-4 on it, and then blow the C-4 when he reached a safe distance. EOD techs get a substantial bonus for doing what they do, along with the fun of blowing stuff up constantly, but in my opinion, no amount of money is worth having to walk up to bombs with your fingers crossed all day.

The EOD Sergeant leaned over to yell at his subordinate in the rear Humvee: "Sergeant Pilke! Get out the RCV!"

"RCV?" I asked.

"Remote control vehicle, sir."

"You guys got a robot?"

"Yes, sir."

I relayed this twist to Peiper, and then walked over to their other Humvee, where they were carefully unloading a large, silver, treaded robot, that looked like a cross between a NASA Rover and Johnny Five from *Short Circuit*. The remote control itself was a massive steel briefcase, complete with fold-out antennas, multiple joysticks, and a view-screen streaming live video feed from the robot's camera. They flipped the robot on, tested it briefly to make sure it was receiving commands from the remote control, and then trundled it over to the bomb, all of us watching intently.

It took a couple of attempts, but they succeeded in yanking out the wire with one of the robot's pincer arms. Nothing happened when it disconnected.

"Okay, do a couple donuts on top of it," the NCO directed.

Incredulous, I watched as the controller guided the robot up onto the bomb, spinning it in place a few times and rolling back and forth.

"How much is that thing worth?" I asked the soldier controlling it.

"Uh, about ten grand."

I suppose it was the safest way of dealing with the bomb, but it was a stubborn IED, and not even a hundred pounds of expensive robot was going to set it off. Then the robot got stuck.

"Shit." The soldier was flipping joysticks, but the robot appeared mired, its tread stuck in something. We could see it straining to move, but no amount of spinning treads was getting it unstuck.

The senior NCO sighed, "Not again. Okay, shut it off and I'll go get it."

He headed for the wire first, staying away from the bomb until he came across the wire. He must have been a curious guy (not a trait that leant itself to survivability in Iraq), because he began to follow the wire south away from the bomb, eventually walking up to the buildings along the edge of Samarra.

Back on my tank, I called Peiper: "You watching this, 2?"

"Roger. Guy's gonna get himself killed."

Armed only with a 9mm pistol, the EOD Sergeant was poking around the buildings, hundreds of meters away from any friendly forces. An insurgent team in the right place could have killed or kidnapped him with their eyes closed. Finally, much to our relief, he followed the wire back to the bomb, cautiously extricating the robot and sauntering back to the Humvee behind my tank.

"Weird thing, sir," he held up some of the wire for me to inspect. "Fishing wire. Won't carry an electric charge, so it wouldn't have worked as a detonator."

"Hmm." I held it, scratching my head. "The explosives are real though?"

"Oh yeah, sir – it's an artillery round."

"Weird," I said. The insurgents we had fought so far didn't generally make rookie mistakes like using the wrong kind of wire. I wondered if perhaps the fishing wire was a decoy, meant to draw us in to investigate, and said as much to the EOD Sergeant.

He took the fishing wire back from me, shrugging. "Could be, sir...we'll probably never know for sure. The wire went a couple more blocks into the city, but I didn't want to go too far in."

"Yeah, we were about to come get you – this is not known as a good neighborhood."

"Okay, we're going to drop some C-4 on the bomb and take care of it. We'll give you a head's up when we're about to blow it."

It took them about five minutes to rig a few blocks of C-4 and hand it off to the robot, which slowly rolled its way back to the bomb. Peiper and I were both getting a little antsy by this point – we'd been sitting there in the same positions, within spitting distance of Samarra, for going on two hours, and our instincts were telling us we had stayed too long. Slowly, haltingly, the robot placed the C-4 in the middle of the mound and made its way back to the Humvee. The senior NCO gave us a countdown, which I relayed over the net to Peiper. I hunkered down in my turret, hatches closed, awaiting the blast.

"...three, two, one!"

Pop.

It was a dud detonator or a faulty set-up: either way, the C-4 did not explode. Now the bomb area was exponentially more dangerous – not only was there an unknown bomb hidden under the earth, there was a block of C-4 sitting on top of it which had failed to detonate. Apparently the NCO was getting impatient, too, because he didn't wait for the robot this time, but instead rigged a small clump of C-4 with another detonator and jogged over to the bomb himself, placing the small piece atop the bigger block of explosive. He was getting it situated just right when a mortar round landed about 75 meters to the right of Staff Sergeant Peiper's tank.

It was a big round, too – we all saw and felt it, and Peiper most of all. He immediately had his driver kick the tank into reverse, backing up fast to clear out of the impact area. This is the correct procedure when receiving indirect fire – immediately displace as fast as possible, so that the enemy is forced to adjust his aim, and try to hit a moving target. Unfortunately, the only direction Peiper could safely move was directly back towards the IED rigged to detonate. As the EOD NCO sprinted back to my tank, I opened my hatch and waved him down.

"Is it ready to blow? We need to clear the fuck out of here!"

"Yeah! It's ready – but I can't blow it with that other tank coming at us – he's going to get too close."

I flipped my radio on. "Green 2, Green 1: short halt right there. I need you to stop in place so we can blow this thing."

"Have you noticed them shooting at me?!"

"If we don't do it now, they'll just be shooting at us again when we come back, over."

I saw him stop the tank.

"That far enough away?" I asked the EOD team leader. He poked his head over my tank's front deck, eye-balling Green 2's position and the IED.

"That'll do," he yelled back to me. "Fire in the hole!"

I dropped down into the turret as the controlled detonation rocked the air around me and buffeted the tank, rocks and sand raining down on us in the wind. I poked back up out of my hatch to see a large crater in the side of the road where the bomb had been. Peiper was already on the move.

"Thanks, guys! Appreciate the help."

The NCO nodded, "See you later, sir – we're out of here." His team was loaded in the Humvees already, and he jumped in as they tore off and headed back to their base. Peiper and I followed suit, getting off the road in a hurry and making for the observation posts farther out of range of the city.

*   *   *

Mortar attacks were a common occurrence during our time out at FOB Rex. About every other day a team of insurgents from Samarra would drive to the edge of the city in a pickup truck, drop a mortar tube into place, and lob half a dozen rounds our way. FOB Rex was small enough that they were never able to get the rounds inside the wire, but it was still a rude awakening whenever it happened. We would respond by dispatching the tanks from both FOB Rex and the observation posts near Samarra in the hopes of catching the truck in a pincer before they scooted back to the safety of the city, but they were usually too quick.

In late August, while Peiper and I were manning the observation posts outside of Samarra, we heard FOB Rex report incoming mortar fire. We started the tanks immediately and roared down to the highway, heading for the general area we knew they would be firing from. At FOB Rex, one of my soldiers on guard duty had noted a white pickup truck high-tailing it out of the area shortly after rounds started impacting. Although probably not the mortar team, he thought their activity unusual enough to send us a radio report – perhaps they were acting as the "spotter" element for the mortars.

At the same instant, Peiper and I spotted two white pickup trucks – one south of the highway heading towards Samarra off-road, the other driving leisurely down the highway towards us. My gunner, Sergeant Cleary, had our tank's sight pointed at the one to the south, and thought he spotted a large metal tube in the back.

I keyed my microphone: "Green 2 this is Green 1, you take the one on the road, I'll go after the one to the south."

"Roger."

I guided my driver off-road and we headed after the truck in the desert. From about a hundred meters away, I waved at them to slow and stop, but they either missed my signal or disregarded it, and kept going.

"Warning shot, sir?" Sergeant Cleary had the main gun tube trained on the fleeing truck.

"Roger. Burst ahead of him."

With its characteristic shredding sound, his machine gun let loose a stream of tracers that arced in front of the truck, kicking up bursts of sand on the dirt track ahead of them. The truck slewed wildly and braked hard, the passengers piling out with their hands in the air. We pulled up next to them, and while I covered them with my rifle, Sergeant Cleary dismounted and searched the truck – they did indeed have a metal tube, but it turned out to be the chimney to a rusty old stove. The rest of the truck was clean.

Back on the road, Staff Sergeant Peiper swerved his tank as he neared the second pickup, bringing the armored vehicle to a stop at an angle fully blocking the road. He pointed the main gun tube firmly at the oncoming truck, whose driver got the message immediately and stopped where he was. Behind him, Sergeant First Class Nicholls and his wing tank pulled up, blocking any escape to the rear.

Peiper and Nicholls were out quickly, pulling the man from the truck and prostrating him on the hot tarmac. When I had my own tank back on the road, I hopped down to see what they had found.

"This guy's fishy, sir," Peiper reported.

"Oh yeah? Anything in the truck?"

"Yeah, wouldn't you know it? A fucking cordless phone, just like the ones we've been finding by the IEDs." Several of the IEDs we had found so far had used a cordless phone as a wireless detonation device, which made them harder to spot (with no wires running away from the site). The technique had become something of a calling card for the IED builder in our area.

Peiper gestured down at the man with his rifle, "And he's got a real attitude, you know? Fucking guy had a smirk on his face when we first pulled him over. When have we ever seen that, you know? Usually they're scared shitless."

Nicholls agreed: "I say we bring him in."

The phone was flimsy circumstantial evidence to say the least, but considering his appearance at the same time we received mortar fire, I agreed with them readily.

"Definitely, let's bring him in. It's not much evidence, but maybe Division's looking for this guy."

And indeed they were. By pulling over a random car – one among thousands we would pull over during the rotation – mostly on a hunch, we ended up bagging one of 1st Infantry Division's top High Value Targets: the brother and trusted lieutenant to the most wanted man in our sector, and a leader of his own insurgent cell.

Headquarters radioed this happy news to us just hours after we sent him back to Mackenzie, and we were all pretty stoked. We got word a couple days later that the story made the Associated Press, but since the nearest reporter was in Baghdad (I assume – we certainly never saw one), they gave the credit to 1-26 Infantry, since Samarra was in their sector. *God damn reporters.*

*   *   *

A few weeks later we got word from Squadron that Major General Batiste, the Commanding General of 1st Infantry Division, was visiting FOBs Wilson and Mackenzie by Humvee, and was also planning on swinging through FOB Rex for a brief visit. We went through the usual preparations – policing up the trash, putting our extra uniform pieces on, double-checking that the guard posts were alert, etc. I was annoyed because this was supposed to be my rest cycle, but as the senior man at FOB Rex, I'd now have to stay awake and give him the tour when he got here.

Sergeant First Class Nicholls was manning the observation posts outside Samarra when the general's convoy appeared, and called me up as we finished our preparations.

"Green 1, this is White 4. I've got visual contact with the General's convoy – ten minute warning, boys. Have fun showing him around."

"Yeah – thanks, White 4," I replied, sarcastically. "How do you always manage to weasel out of these things?"

"Years of experience."

I smiled. I was about to put my radio microphone down and head over to the guard post by the main gate when I heard Nicholls on the radio again, calling his wingman.

"White 3, White 4 – you seeing this?"

White 3 answered quickly: "Shit – yeah, roger. Starting up my tank now."

"Green 1, White 4."

I keyed the net again. "Green 1, over."

"This is White 4: General Batiste just missed the turn and is

77

headed straight into Samarra, over."

"Green 1: acknowledged. We're starting up here, too, leaving in two minutes." *Perfect: a two-star general driving into the heart of insurgent-held Samarra with four lightly-armed Humvees.* I flipped off my helmet and relayed this news to SGT Cleary, who swore and kicked our crew awake. Peiper had overheard the conversation and was readying his tank, as usual ready far quicker than I was able. As we started for the gate, churning up clouds of soft sand, Nicholls came on the net.

"Stand down, Green. He's figured it out and is turning back out of the city now, headed your way."

"Roger…thanks White."

I sighed in relief, the mental image of our tanks fighting their way through hordes of insurgents fading gratefully. The last thing I wanted was being partially responsible for landing a General on Al Jazeera surrounded by masked insurgents.

The Commanding General didn't show it when he visited, but he was pretty much appalled at the living conditions out at FOB Rex. We had put a lot of work into the place by this point – we tripled the wire around the outpost, fortified the entrance, replaced the tents with trailers to live in (though without generators and air conditioning, we never got around to using them), and cleaned up the trash that blew in on a daily basis from the neighboring countryside. Iraqis don't have trash collection or designated dumps – they burn their trash, or just toss it wherever, which means that it blows all over the place in the wind and the whole country smells like a landfill. The farming and lack of sewage in most places don't help the odor situation, either – you get used to it after a while, but most of us found the stench over-powering when we first arrived in country.

So after the months of work we'd put in, rumor made its way down to us that FOB Rex was officially condemned and scheduled for replacement. We were both relieved and slightly annoyed – *why couldn't they have realized that it was a shithole <u>before</u> we spent months here?* About the same time another piece of news reached us, which I had the job of breaking to my soldiers. I pulled everyone together at the retrans site in the early evening as we finished up an MRE meal. I looked around at my men – they were dusty and tired, their uniforms stained with tank grease and gun oil and sweat, yet they were smiling and laughing, enjoying the cooler air and freedom to relax for a few hours. Some of them had been home for leave already, the rest, like me, were still waiting our turn. Every single one of them could have told me, precisely and without hesitation, the number of days we had been in theater, and the number that still remained in our 12-month tour. We had recently passed the halfway point.

I took a deep breath, and shook my head, chagrined. "It's bad news, guys." I paused. "The Department of Defense has extended 1st Infantry Division's tour by a month."

The smiles and laughter disappeared abruptly. Someone spat, the impact kicking up a small cloud of dust. Someone else swore quietly. We were all thinking the same thing – this meant another month away from our families, another month of long hours and crappy conditions, and another month in harm's way. And it meant we were back to being less than halfway done. They asked a few questions, I told them what I knew about why it was being done – something to do with troop levels and rotation schedules – it didn't really matter. In our own ways, we each put it behind us, said "fuck it," and went back about our jobs. In light of other deployment extensions (for the 2007-2008 "surge," the standard Army tour was increased from 12 to 15 months), our own extension was minor, but it was still an ass-kicker at the time. 1st Armored Division got it far worse, however: their tour was extended to 15 months *while they were in the process of returning to Germany.* Some poor bastards were already home, relaxing with their families, and they were told to pack their gear and get back on the plane.

CHAPTER SEVEN

"I love the fucking Army, and the Army loves fucking me."
-Graffiti in a porta-john at FOB Mackenzie

We knew that the Cajun Mousetrap operations were just a precursor to a bigger mission to retake Samarra, but an operation of that scale would take some time to coordinate, so in the interim we returned to the drudgery of our observation post missions at FOB Rex. In September, I was back at FOB Mackenzie on a 24 hour rest rotation, stripping down for my first shower in days, when a runner from the command post knocked on my door and informed me that Captain Hoffman wanted to see me immediately. I sighed and pulled my gear back on, then jogged over to the bunker where our troop had set up shop.

"Sir – you wanted to see me?"

"Vince Taylor's going in for surgery, and he's not coming back," he told me.

Vince was platoon leader of 1st / Red Platoon, one of our two scout platoons. He had deployed to Iraq with an injured ankle that should have been operated on months before, but he chose to ignore the pain to be with his men when they went downrange. It was an admirable decision, but the injury was getting worse, and he was worried that his infirmity would put his soldiers at risk in a critical situation. When he could no longer hide his limp, he was ordered to see a doctor, who sent him back to Germany to get operated on immediately. Before he left, Vince had managed to convince Captain

Hoffman and the Squadron Commander to leave his platoon leader slot open for a short while, so that if the doctors in Germany told him he could safely put off the surgery, or if the surgery and recovery were exceptionally quick, he might return to his old job. That was no longer a possibility, and it left his platoon without an officer.

Captain Hoffman continued: "The squadron commander and I want you to take over his platoon."

My heart beat faster – getting a scout platoon was a highly sought after promotion, but also an entirely new challenge, and one I would have to tackle while running combat missions.

"Thank you, sir. I hope I'm up to it. When do I take over?"

"In about a week," he said. "Red Platoon's acting as Squadron quick reaction force right now, so there's no big rush. Second Lieutenant Takashi will take over your platoon – he's been in Headquarters Troop for a few months now, waiting for a platoon. Work out a timeline to sign over your tank platoon equipment to him."

"Roger."

"In the meantime, I want you to take him with you next time you go out to the retrans site, do a good solid battle handoff with him, show him the ropes, the whole deal."

"Okay, roger, sir."

A week gave me very little time to get things in order to hand off my current responsibilities, much less start learning my new ones. I called over to Squadron headquarters to find out where Lieutenant Takashi was, so I could introduce myself and we could start planning for the handoff. Next I went to the motor pool to find Staff Sergeant Peiper and let him know what was happening. I found our crews changing a road wheel on one of the tanks.

"Hey, Sergeant...got some news."

"Oh yeah, sir? Did they finally decide to stop sending us out to FOB Rex?"

I shook my head ruefully. "No, sorry – we're still going out. But we'll be taking your new platoon leader with us tomorrow. I'm taking over Red platoon in a week."

"No shit? Who's the new guy?"

"A guy called Takashi."

"Have you met him?" He would be Peiper's new wingman, so Peiper was anxious to know more about him – particularly how he might handle the fact that his platoon sergeant (Dude) was such a mess.

"Yeah, I just talked to him for a while. I let him know about Dude and told him to listen to you and Kean if he wants to get out of here in one piece."

Peiper snorted at the mention of Dude, but I could see he was still uneasy.

"Anyway, it doesn't matter," I said. "You and Kean run this platoon, he's just along for the ride. He'll learn that. I'm not worried about the platoon as long as you two are around."

"Yeah. We saved your ass, that's for sure."

I laughed. "You did, no question." I put out my hand. "Seriously, though – thanks for everything you taught me. I'm only getting a scout platoon because you and Kean kept me steered in the right direction. And I couldn't have asked for a better wingman. It's been an honor."

He shook my hand – I knew he hated serious moments like this, but I wanted him to know how much I appreciated him as a mentor and friend.

"You were a real good platoon leader, sir."

"Thanks – that means a lot to me." And it did – the typical officer / NCO relationship is based on a lot of good-natured rivalry and banter, insults being the most common form of communication. A good officer will instinctively know that he's doing well as a leader despite these insults from his NCOs, but it was good to hear it from a respected veteran like Peiper.

"I'll miss you guys," I told him. "Stay out of trouble."

He grinned at me, his eyes sparkling mischievously: "Who, me?"

I was heading back to my room to see if I couldn't take that shower when another one of the soldiers from our troop operations center sauntered up.

"Green 1! Bulldawg 6 needs to see you right now."

I frowned. "Damn it, I was just there! About what?"

"Dunno, sir, he just told me to come get you ASAP."

I headed back towards the troop bunker. I was more than a little pissed – with less than 24 hours back at base before my tanks were due out at the retrans site again, every hour was precious. I made my way to the bunker, pushing in the door painted in cavalry red and white, and knocked on Captain Hoffman's office door again.

"Come in. Oh, Platt – good. Change of mission. Red platoon's been attached to Anvil Troop for a raid tomorrow night. You'll be leading them on that raid."

I was completely caught by surprise: not just that I would take over immediately, but that my first mission would be a raid – the most complex and demanding mission in our bag of tricks – and with another troop, no less. I smiled wryly: "It's a good thing Red Platoon's got good NCOs, sir."

In the back of my mind, the guilty, lazy part of me was celebrating the happy fact that I wouldn't be back at FOB Rex in 24 hours. Hoffman was still talking to me.

"Sorry, can you say again, sir?"

"I said Anvil 6 is having the raid operations order tomorrow at 1000. Represent Bulldawg Troop well, Red 1."

Red 1: my new call-sign. I smiled – despite everything, it had a nice ring to it.

"Yessir."

I was worried about my new platoon sergeant – Sergeant First Class Martin – and the other NCOs in 1st Platoon, though. I wasn't sure how they would take to relinquishing control of the platoon, after nearly two months of successfully running things on their own without an officer around. In 4th Platoon, it had taken me a few months of working with Peiper and Kean to earn their respect and build a strong working relationship, and though my reputation as a competent leader preceded me from that job, I knew there would be a similar "break-in" period as the Red Platoon NCOs and I got used to working with each other – except that this time, we'd have to do that in combat. I knocked on the door of Sergeant First Class Martin's room.

"Come in."

He was lying on his bed, watching a DVD on his laptop and munching some chips.

"Hey, Sergeant Martin."

"What's up, P-squared?"

"Well…" I hesitated. "Bulldawg 6 just told me I'm your new platoon leader, starting now."

"No shit? Good: now I don't have to go to all his bullshit meetings anymore – you can."

I laughed – I shouldn't have worried about Martin. Probably the most universally-liked NCO in Squadron, Sergeant First Class Martin was as easy-going as he was calm and firm under pressure. Soft-spoken in comparison to a lot of his peers, when Martin chose to speak up, soldiers of all ranks listened closely. An experienced Bradley Master Gunner, he had a knack for developing young soldiers that had resulted in a tightly-knit, disciplined platoon.

"Naw, congratulations, sir," he stood and shook my hand. "It's good to have you."

Martin stuck his head out the door and sent one of our scouts over to find our two section sergeants, so that we could hold a platoon meeting to discuss the upcoming raid. Staff Sergeant Neathery and Staff Sergeant Barnes soon showed up, sauntering into the room and stacking their rifles by the door.

"Well...a brand new platoon leader." Neathery said, looking me up and down appraisingly.

"Shit. Why couldn't they have given us Mongo?" Barnes muttered, implying I was his last choice to be their platoon leader.

I laughed, but before I could retaliate Martin jumped in to my defense.

"Easy now, easy – someone's gotta do all the paperwork around here."

The ice broken, we set down to discussing the platoon. It had worked well for me back in my tank platoon, so I started the same way with the three of them.

"Look – I don't know jack about scout operations, so I'm going to be leaning on you guys for a bit until I get on my feet, okay? To start with, how do we operate?"

"What, doctrinally, or here in Iraq?" Martin asked, chuckling.

I shrugged. "Both."

"Doctrinally, you've got your six vehicles, which you can split into Alpha Section – the 1, 2, and 3 tracks, and Bravo Section – 4, 5, and 6." Martin told me.

"Okay, like the two sections in the tank platoons."

"This ain't like tanking, sir," Barnes corrected, offended.

"You can also split off a Charlie Section, giving you three sections of two Brads each," Martin continued.

"And here in Iraq?" I asked.

"You know how it is – doctrine goes out the window. We usually roll with two tracks. 1 goes with 5, 2 goes with 3, and I roll with 6,"

Martin explained. "But we mix it up, too."

"Dismounts?" I prompted.

Barnes snorted with disgust. "We're supposed to have at least two, if not three, per track. *Supposed to.* With you here now, we've got 25 swinging dicks in the platoon – so that would be about one dismount per track, after you account for each Bradley needing a gunner, commander, and driver. But with R&R and details like sending a guy to run the sign-in sheet at the fucking internet center, and another guy to wash dishes, that works out to…not enough. We shut down a track every now and then to scrape together more dismounts."

It was the same story as in my tank platoon – we hadn't been filled at 100% strength until five months *after* we arrived in Iraq, but that still added up to less than 100% when you factored in R&R leave and soldiers on details. We talked for a while more about where they had been operating, what the enemy situation was like in the sector, and what the plan for the following day's raid would look like. At the end of it, I felt slightly more comfortable, though I knew I still had a lot to learn. As we wrapped things up, Barnes switched subjects, and asked me if I was married.

"Nope – engaged. College sweetheart."

"You got a picture?"

I pulled out my wallet and fished out a worn photo of my fiancée, handing it over. They inspected it in turn. Barnes – ever the loudmouth wiseass – couldn't resist commenting.

"She's hot, sir!"

I wasn't quite sure how to respond to that. He pressed on.

"You better hurry up and marry her soon. She's back home just dodging dicks right now."

∗   ∗   ∗

The raid I would be leading Red Platoon on for my first mission as a scout platoon leader was an attempt to capture the #1 High Value Target in Samarra, an Iraqi insurgent leader who had supposedly called for a meeting among his subordinates at a house south of the city, along the Tigris. I wrote out my operations order that evening, then called the men together the following morning, anxious to make a good impression. After briefing them on the raid, I quizzed a few of the soldiers on the key details, and then turned them over to their NCOs.

"How was that?" I asked Sergeant First Class Martin, as our scouts started to head out to prepare for the mission.

"Fine," he shrugged. "Don't sweat it."

A dark-haired Sergeant walked up to us and stuck out his hand.

"Sergeant Wasser – I'm your new gunner, sir."

I shook his hand, "So you're my babysitter, huh?"

Martin slapped Wasser on the back. "Wasser here knows his way around the turret – he'll take care of you," he told me.

"Yeah, speaking of which – can you take me out to the motor pool and walk me through some stuff on the Bradley?" I asked Wasser.

He nodded eagerly, "Sure, sir. We're headed out to prep the tracks now."

One big perk of running a scout platoon, I discovered, was the fact that we had two Humvees assigned to us, which meant that we could drive to the motor pool instead of walking the hot, sweaty mile or so. At the Bradleys, I met my new driver, a young Specialist known to all as "Scooter." Scooter wore coke-bottle glasses thick enough to cause me slight alarm.

"What's your vision like, Scooter?"

"20-20, as long as I've got these on, sir!"

"Keep 'em on, then," I chuckled.

From his driver's station, Scooter lowered the ramp at the back of the passenger compartment, and we walked up it into the rear of the vehicle. The M3 Bradley is designed both as a fighting vehicle in its own right, and an armored personnel carrier. In its infantry configuration, it carries up to six soldiers in the back, on two narrow benches lining the walls of the compartment. In its cavalry configuration, the right-hand bench is replaced by a storage rack holding extra anti-tank missile rounds. The rear end of the vehicle is a thick steel-plate ramp with a door in it – dismounts can either go in and out through the door, or the driver can lower the whole ramp to the ground, which is hinged at its base. The vehicle's turret sits at the front of the passenger compartment, and is accessible via a door that the commander and gunner can awkwardly squeeze through. The door is closed for safety during operations – otherwise, someone might get a limb caught in the spinning turret mechanism. The driver's seat is accessible both through its own external hatch on the front left of the vehicle, and by crawling through the "hell-hole," a narrow crawlspace next to the turret which connects the driver's station to the rear compartment.

The gunner and Bradley commander sit side-by-side up in the turret, with the gunner on the left. Each man has his own hatch in the roof above, and his own controls for operating the turret and weapons systems. The Bradley's main armament is the 25mm Bushmaster, a cannon capable of firing 200 rounds per minute, either singly or in sustained bursts. The gunner, moreover, can choose what type of round he wants to fire, and switch between the two on the fly. As in the tank, the two main rounds are AP (armor-piercing) and HE (high explosive). In Iraq, we used AP rounds only to punch holes in walls the enemy was using for cover – HE was the killing round. Because the gun is much smaller than a tank's, it rotates in the turret faster and has a wider range of movement, making it a far more effective weapon for close-quarters urban combat. As on the tank, the Bradley also packs a co-axial machine gun mounted alongside the main gun.

The weapons package is rounded out with a TOW missile launcher mounted on the left side of the turret, which is raised into position before firing. The TOW (Tube-launched, Optically-tracked, Wire-guided) missile can destroy armored targets more than two miles away, and because of its wire guidance system, the gunner can track moving targets, adjusting the course of the missile while it's in flight.

Most of this I knew already, so Wasser walked me through some of the finer details of operating on the vehicle – tips and tricks, safety measures, evacuation procedures, a quick-and-dirty run through the turret controls and gunnery techniques. I filed away as much as I could remember, and took the chance to position some of my equipment in the turret – maps and pens, laminated reports, the UAV and satellite photos of the area where the night's raid was taking place, and my GPS unit.

As dusk fell the following night, we loaded into the Bradleys outside Squadron headquarters, my NCOs talking to their crews, checking weapons and equipment, quizzing them on their roles in the night's mission. On cue from Anvil 6 (Captain Black, the Anvil Troop commander), we lined up and rolled out, our long line of vehicles rumbling through the gathering dark. It was a twenty minute ride to the target area, and as we approached we received updated intelligence from Squadron HQ, who was watching a live video feed from a drone flying above the river.

"Anvil, this is Saber X-Ray: we're observing a large group of civilian vehicles at the target site, clustered around what appears to be a tent."

Our intelligence team had estimated an enemy force of up to 150 guards to protect the high level leadership that was supposedly at the meeting, and this big group of cars seemed to confirm that assessment. We made the final turn onto the peninsula where the house was located, picking up speed and switching to black-out drive, headlights off for maximum "surprise" (never mind the ungodly racket 30 tracked vehicles were making). Barnes, in the lead of our platoon, found the side road we had picked to deploy along, and we split off from the main column as Anvil Red drove into the heart of the complex. Our job was to be the outer cordon, while Anvil's scouts cleared the buildings. As we set in place and I began marking down the locations of my different vehicles to report to Anvil X-Ray, I kept my ears open for the sound of a firefight. It was eerily quiet.

During the first five to ten minutes of a raid, the clearing teams are generally too busy to report frequently. I learned over time to be patient and let my men work, but oftentimes headquarters would get impatient and demand an update, curious to know if the raid was successful or not. In this case, since Major Randall (the Squadron Operations Officer) was on the ground, they were more patient knowing he would be monitoring the situation closely himself. For those of us on the perimeter, though, we spent a solid 20 minutes wondering what was happening in amongst the buildings. *Had we caught the insurgent leader?*

Finally, Major Randall came on the net and told me to move to his location – the main house at the center of the property. Once there, I hopped down and jogged into the house, which was being casually guarded by several Anvil Troopers. Major Randall and Captain Black were being harangued by an older man who was not at all pleased about his house being tossed by surly cavalrymen late at night. The "insurgent conference" from our intelligence report was in reality the final night of prayers following a funeral for his mother. No insurgents, no 150 guards. Major Randall saw me, politely excused himself from the old man's diatribe, and motioned me to the side.

"Darkhorse is reporting there's some guy hiding in the weeds along the river just north of here. Go check it out."

"Yes, sir."

Outside, I hopped back onto my track, keying the net to relay the news of the raid to my platoon.

"Green, this is...correction! *Red*, this is *Red* 1, situation report follows, over." I was going to catch hell for that from my new platoon – after six months of calling myself "Green 1," it had become totally reflexive. After a few sarcastic transmissions about color-blindness from several of my Bradley commanders, I gave them the update and then asked Staff Sergeant Neathery, my new wingman – Red 5, to guide his track to my location. As we moved north of the house, peering down the steep slope to the river, I switched to the Squadron frequency.

"Any Darkhorse element, this is Bulldawg Red 1 on the Squadron net."

"This is Darkhorse 22, go ahead Bulldawg." As always, the helicopter pilot's voice sounded oddly muffled, as his microphone struggled to dampen the background noise of the rotors.

"Roger, my 5 element and I are moving north of the objective to investigate possible insurgent hiding along the riverbank, over."

"This is Darkhorse 22, roger! I've been trying to get Anvil Troop to find this guy, but they couldn't see him and bailed on me. I've got eyes on his location now, I'll talk you in. Be advised: Darkhorse is ten minutes to 'bingo' on fuel, and we do *not* have another Air Weapons Team on standby, over."

In aviator terminology, "bingo" meant that their remaining fuel was only enough to return to base – it was the literal point-of-no-return for helicopters. If we didn't find this guy in the next ten minutes, we would lose him. We stopped on the road when we reached the area Darkhorse was orbiting. With all six vehicles in the fight tonight, we had only one dismount between our two tracks, however – Sergeant Shore, one of our two platoon marksmen – so Staff Sergeant Neathery dismounted along with him, taking a dismount radio. The two of them side-stepped down the steep bank, disappearing into the thick reeds at the edge.

"Red 1, Red 5."

"This is Red 1."

"Yeah, roger – can you have Darkhorse spotlight the guy, over?"

I relayed his request to the pilots, who dutifully flipped on their powerful, nose-mounted spotlight, training it on the man in the water.

"Okay, this is 5 – we've got eyes on him, but he's like halfway out into the river – I don't think we're going to be able to get him without going swimming, over."

Shit. A few weeks prior, a soldier elsewhere in Iraq had drowned swimming in the Tigris, which is both deep and swift-moving. The result was that a high-level directive had just been published reminding soldiers they were not to swim *for any reason,* recreational or operational, while in Iraq.

"Yeah, no swimming, 5." I thought hard, checking my watch – seven minutes to "bingo," and there was an excellent chance we would lose this guy for good the minute the pilots took the spotlight off him to return to base.

My earpiece crackled to life. "Red 1, Darkhorse 22."

"This is Red 1."

"Roger, we monitor that he's too far out of reach – we think we've spotted a boat about 100 meters south of your dismounts' location."

Well, I thought, *that safety directive hadn't said anything about boats.* It would be a clear violation of the intent of the rule, but it wasn't *technically* prohibited, as far as I knew. I called Neathery.

"Red 5, you monitor?"

"Roger, we're moving."

They found the boat, but it lacked a motor, oars, or paddles of any kind. Neathery and Shore were determined not to let Darkhorse down, however. They got the boat in the water, towed it up the bank to the area nearest the swimmer, and got in. Using the reeds, they pulled themselves close to him, but as they got farther out into the river, the current began to catch them, propelling them away from the man. They began to paddle with their hands, but could not move the boat upstream against the swift current. With their arms tiring fast, they realized they were not going to reach him, so Neathery and Shore started to point the boat back towards the bank, abandoning the man in an attempt to avoid getting swept further out into the river.

What Darkhorse did next became something of a legend in the air troops, and cemented a close working relationship between Bulldawg and Darkhorse, which continued throughout our tour. Seeing the two scouts try so hard and come so close to success, the Darkhorse pilot decided he wasn't going to let them fail. With his aircraft at "bingo," he stopped flying in a circle around the area and came in for a close hover over the water, just downstream of Neathery and Shore in the boat. Angling his blades just right, he used the powerful downdraft of the rotors to physically push the boat back upstream toward the swimmer. Neathery and Shore, at first totally confused at what the hell was going on, later couldn't stop laughing about how amazing a maneuver it had been. They were at the swimmer in moments, and hauled him in, waving to Darkhorse as they did so.

"Red 1, Darkhorse 22 – your dismounts have the swimmer, Darkhorse is returning to base for refuel at this time, over."

"Roger, Darkhorse – good news, thanks for the assist."

"Thank *you* guys for coming over to help."

I honestly don't remember what happened to the man we captured – I think he was probably detained for a while and then released, since we had no evidence on him other than the fact that he was actively trying to escape the target location. We saved his life, however – he had been out in the water so long that he was approaching hypothermia when they hauled him out, and Sergeant Shore saw him go under several times as they approached him.

My new platoon ended up with the only success stories of the mission, though little of it was due to my efforts. While Red 5 and I were off playing Coast Guard, Staff Sergeant Barnes acted on an earlier Darkhorse report of suspicious activity from a small house near his location on the outer cordon. Searching the house – whose occupants had left while he was parked on cordon duty – they found an AK-47 with a bandolier of ammunition, and an RPG launcher with several rounds. It would have been an auspicious start to my career as a scout platoon leader, except for the fact that my Bradley broke down messily a mile or so short of FOB Mackenzie's main gate on our return march. It wasn't my fault, of course, but I never quite lived that one down.

I went to see Major Randall the following day, seeking his advice on putting Neathery and Shore in for an award, along with the resourceful Darkhorse crew.

"I believe if you check the after action report, you'll see that the man was simply pulled out of the water by soldiers on the riverbank,

Lieutenant. Do you know why it says that?"

I frowned. "No, sir…?"

"Because U.S. forces in Iraq are prohibited from using watercraft without training or proper safety equipment," he told me sternly.

"Oh," I said, disheartened. "Roger, sir."

"Nice work, though," he said, winking.

*   *   *

I had thought it would be a long time before I saw Samarra again, but I was wrong. Soon after the raid with Anvil Troop, Squadron sent us back to Bulldawg Troop with orders to secure three new traffic control points scheduled for construction on the main roads to the south, northeast, and northwest of Samarra. The plan called for a massive amount of construction, which would be accomplished by Army Engineers: each checkpoint would be several hundred meters long, a cement fortress of ten-foot-tall jersey barriers with machine gun towers and designated search areas off the main road. They were well-designed, but they were also a stone's throw from the city itself, easily within small arms fire range, and anyone manning them would make juicy targets for snipers and mortar fire. Samarra was still a "no-go" zone for U.S. forces, so parking a couple Engineer platoons on its outskirts to build these fortifications was likely to draw all kinds of unpleasant attention.

And it certainly did. White Platoon drew the first security watch on the checkpoints, overwatching the Engineers as they arrived and began clearing the area around the first site, dropping cement blocks into place, and generally making a big racket and an even bigger target. Out at FOB Rex, we used to see about ten rounds of mortar fire a week being shot at us. In 30 straight hours of construction operations, White Platoon reported no less than 30 incoming rounds, which landed with increasing accuracy but miraculously failed to cause any casualties.

They sent the Engineers out the following day as planned, and also sent two Apache attack helicopters to orbit the area as additional security. The insurgents knew their business, however, and merely set up their mortar tubes several blocks in, behind buildings or inside buildings without roofs, and continued to shoot undisturbed. Finally, on the third day, some senior officers showed up to tour the construction sites, and while we were showing them around, they took both sniper fire and several mortar rounds. This was enough to convince them that the plan needed a bit of revision: the Engineers began packing it in and we moved back to FOB Mackenzie.

They didn't concede the point fully, however, and requested that while the plan was revised, the sites be guarded – from a safe distance – so that the locals didn't make off with all the expensive construction materials left behind. Two of my Bradley commanders, Staff Sergeants Neathery and Romano, drew this task. On the morning of the fourth day, they set their two Bradleys in position several hundred meters north of the checkpoint. The firing started soon.

In an uncharacteristic display of courage, perhaps emboldened by their success at driving off the bulk of our forces, the insurgents decided to take on the two Bradleys in a stand-up fight. They opened up with rifles and machine guns from long distance, taking up positions in the buildings on the northern edge of the city. Even from several hundred meters away, they were able to score some hits on the vehicles, the bullets ricocheting off the armor and sending an adrenaline jolt through the crews of Red 5 and 6. The two men started their vehicles and closed their hatches, scanning the buildings to begin to identify targets as bullets continued to harass them. Red 5 reported the contact, and within several minutes a flight of two Apaches was lifting off the tarmac at FOB Speicher to the north, inbound for Samarra at high speed. Back at FOB Mackenzie, word reached me that my soldiers were in a fight, and since I couldn't join them, I jogged over to the troop command post to listen in on the radio.

Neathery and Romano could not identify targets from their location, and they weren't going to just sit there without striking back, so they pushed forward and approached the highway between them and the city. The firing from the buildings intensified, bullets clattering off the armor at a steady rate. At the same time, Red 5 and 6 saw men moving from the buildings under cover of the machine gun fire, heading to the flanks of the Bradleys in what was clearly a planned, coordinated maneuver. The men were dressed in black, carrying Soviet rocket-propelled grenade (RPG) launchers, and they moved in pairs – a gunner and a loader carrying spare ammunition.

Red 5 and 6 knew at once that they were fighting a more

experienced enemy. Intelligence analysis following the fight identified them as foreign jihadists, likely veterans of fighting in Afghanistan or Palestine, approximately 50 in number. Though the small-arms fire was heavy, the RPG teams posed the most significant threat to Neathery and Romano, whose gunners immediately opened fire on the insurgents as they moved out of the cover of the buildings.

Within seconds, two of the RPG teams had been destroyed with accurate 25mm cannon fires, the explosive shells tearing through the exposed fighters. The gunners then turned their attention to the buildings and began engaging targets as they appeared in windows, doors, and on rooftops. Neathery's crew killed a particularly well-concealed machine gunner with a TOW missile round, firing the missile through the building's window; his gunner saw their target get ripped in half by the force of the blast. At about this time, the Apaches arrived on station, hovering over the Bradleys in support and checking in with Red 5 on the radio.

The focus in combat is always the fight on the ground – though air assets can significantly affect the outcome of a battle, the main effort is on the ground. For this reason, aviation units fall under the tactical command of ground forces when the two coordinate, and it is up to the senior man on the ground (in this case, Staff Sergeant Neathery) to figure out how to employ those air assets. There is no real playbook for this scenario, however – almost all of the Army's Field Manuals detail how units at larger levels should fight a similarly-equipped enemy army. Neathery decided to maximize cooperation between the two units, attaching one Apache to Red 6 to work with, and keeping the other for himself. With each man talking directly to the pilot hovering near him, they were thus able to coordinate their fires with devastating effect.

The Apaches opened up with 30mm chain gun fire and Hellfire missiles, gutting several buildings and wreaking havoc on the enemy's front line positions. The fight continued to intensify, however, as insurgents began firing RPGs at long range, arcing the rounds over the rooftops toward the Bradleys like indirect mortar rounds. The insurgents also set up a 120mm mortar and began lobbing rounds at the Bradleys with distressing accuracy, at one point placing a round just 50 meters short of Red 5's position. A direct hit would have destroyed either vehicle, killing all inside.

Apaches are fearsomely armed, but not well-equipped for a sustained gunfight. Within a short period of time, each gunship expended its full ammo load. The Apache lead pilot came on the radio.

"Red 5, Gunfighter 5: we need to return to base to rearm."

"This is Red 5, roger."

"This is Gunfighter 5 – we'll be back in 10 minutes, I guarantee it! Just hold them off, we'll be right back!"

They were as good as their word, and the support crews at FOB Speicher had the two birds rearmed and refueled in record time, juggling rockets and links of chain gun ammo like a pit crew at full tilt. Red 5 and 6 continued to hold their ground under fire, and in the meantime, the Air Force liaison team at Squadron headquarters had an F-18 fighter jet rerouted from Fallujah, which took up position several thousand feet over the city, waiting for a target from the ground. Red 5 was happy to oblige, and as the Apaches moved well back, he picked a building on the edge of the city from which the small arms fire was heaviest.

"Red 5, Bulldawg X-Ray: air support requests you mark the target with 25mm fire, over."

"This is Red 5, acknowledged. Marking target now."

He fired a sustained burst of 25mm rounds into the building, the explosions from which were readily apparent to the pilot making a low pass over the city. The pilot locked the target into his targeting computer, banked hard, and then climbed to altitude again, lining himself up for the bombing run. Several thousand feet below, the Bradleys braced for the impact, eyes fixed on the building, which still showed multiple muzzle flashes from insurgents firing at their position. Several hundred yards away, a civilian car had inexplicably decided to brave the firefight to enter the city, a fact which no one noticed until after we had a chance to check out the targeting footage from the F-18. That guy had a hell of a shock that afternoon.

500 pounds of high explosive hit with a bright white flash, jets of smoke and debris streaking out of the cement building far into the air above. The small arms fire halted abruptly, those insurgents not caught within the blast radius concussed or temporarily deafened by the explosion. Realizing they were inviting further disaster by remaining on the edge of the city, the survivors quickly regrouped and retreated, but soon began opening fire on the Bradleys and

Apaches once again.

It took them several minutes to locate the insurgents' fallback positions, but Gunfighter 5 managed to do so after side-slipping several hundred yards to the west and training his thermal sights down a main street running south through the city before him.

"Red 5, Gunfighter 5, I've located the source of that small arms fire, over."

"This is Red 5, roger – we're moving to your location."

"Gunfighter 5, roger – insurgents are using the Golden Mosque for cover. I can identify multiple gunmen behind a low wall on the perimeter of the mosque. Do I have permission to fire, over?"

Neathery paused, momentarily stumped. On the one hand, it is hammered into the soldier that his job is to gain and maintain contact, and once the initiative has been seized, to continue to assault enemy forces. These enemy were better-trained and more dangerous than any we had yet faced, but they were also losing, and everyone in the battle sensed this. On the other hand, it had been made crystal clear to us during our training that certain things in Islamic culture were completely unacceptable: mistreatment of women, disrespect towards the Koran, and anything that violated the sanctity of mosques, in particular. Violations of these principles would not only land us in serious hot water with our chain of command, they were also likely to incite widespread violence from the local populace.

Neathery erred on the side of caution, and relayed the latest situation to the troop commander, who, in turn, passed the buck on to Squadron headquarters, knowing full well that such a decision was well above his pay grade, too. While the enemy continued to fire, and the scouts and helicopters waited, Major Randall at Squadron headquarters sent the report on up to Division headquarters with a request for a speedy reply. But it didn't stop there.

Even Division wasn't willing to weigh in on this one – it had all the potential for a major public relations backlash. The assistant division commander picked up the secure telephone and dialed the number for Multi-National Forces Iraq Command in Baghdad, and succeeded in getting the highest ranking man in Iraq, Lieutenant General Metz, on the phone in a matter of minutes. General Metz mulled it over, and gave them permission to fire.

By the time word was relayed back to the forces in contact, however, the insurgents had gotten over their suicidal tendencies, and backed off from the fight, withdrawing farther back into the city and out of contact. It was still a hell of a day for coalition forces, however: our Bradleys had an estimated 15-20 kills between them, and the Apaches posted a similar number. In the back of our minds, however, we all knew that major operations to retake Samarra were just around the corner, and if all the insurgents we faced then were as hardcore and well-trained as those Red 5 and 6 had fought, it didn't bode well for us.

*   *   *

My platoon was attached back to Anvil Troop the next week, and we soon began to hear rumors that the mission to retake Samarra was a "go." Anvil's commander, Captain Black, hinted at it in his troop meetings, and when all of the troop commanders were called to Squadron headquarters along with their Fire Support Officers and key operations center personnel, we knew it meant that Squadron would be issuing its official operations order. We also knew it would be a pretty epic operation incorporating most of the 1st Infantry Division's combat forces, on a scale not yet attempted in our deployment. Some units would be entering the city and clearing it block by block, and the first units into the city would face stiff resistance and probably suffer casualties, but we didn't know which units would be picked for which tasks.

While it felt as if a lot had happened since taking over as scout platoon leader, in reality, it had been less than a month. I was still getting to know my men and my NCOs' different strengths, and I still felt like a complete rookie when it came to scout operations. Much of what we had done so far was similar to what I had done in my tank platoon, but the Samarra mission would be wildly different – I understood how to maneuver tanks in a battle, but I was sure I was missing a whole book's worth of valuable knowledge about how to employ Bradleys effectively. We reported to the Anvil Troop operations center several hours after the squadron order was completed, during which time Captain Black had written up his troop-level order. I expected that we would be given a few days' time to prep for the Samarra mission, but Captain Black dispelled that misconception immediately.

"Operation Baton Rouge is a 'go.' We're going into Samarra

tomorrow night."

Even though more time to prepare would not have made much difference, I felt my stomach drop.

"…and we're going to be the first ones in."

The Division plan was fairly complex, but our squadron's piece of it was actually quite simple. 1-4 CAV, in true cavalry fashion, would be the first elements into Samarra, starting at midnight the following night. Our mission was to conduct simultaneous raids – Charlie Troop in the north, Anvil to the southeast – on the perimeter of the city, not with the objective to capture any specific insurgents or clear any buildings, just to drive up and give the bees' nest a good whack, as it were. After destroying any enemy encountered, we would then conduct a "passage of lines" operation (it sounds fancy, but it just means letting another unit pass through your location and take over the fight) with 1-77 Armor and 1-18 Infantry, whose job it would be to undertake the exhausting and thankless task of clearing the city, house by house and room by room. 1-26 Infantry would be attacking the city from the west across the main Tigris bridge, and all three battalions would push their way inwards until they met at the center of the city, near the city's famous Golden Mosque.

Meanwhile, as soon as the passage of lines was completed, Squadron would establish a cordon surrounding the city, in order to prevent any movement into or out of the city – the idea was that there would be a line of vehicles positioned in a giant arc around the entire city, from one edge of the Tigris to the other. That cordon was to remain in place for no more than three days, until the city had been cleared and 1-26 Infantry was ready to resume patrols in the now-pacified city.

"Bulldawg Troop is the main effort for the screen line," Captain Black said, looking at me, "So you'll revert to your troop following the passage of lines. Captain Hoffman is having his operations order brief in an hour."

Great, I thought. *Not one, but two commanders and two different orders. Just what I need to keep things simple and easy.*

Captain Black wrapped up his order, paused for questions, and then dismissed us. I headed over to my own troop headquarters to hear what the next phase of the operation would look like.

Captain Hoffman, it turned out, was going on R&R leave, which left his second in command, First Lieutenant O'Brien, in charge of the troop. All of us found this a little odd – Baton Rouge was clearly the biggest operation of our tour, the most dangerous and complex mission we would undertake. I don't know if Captain Hoffman asked to postpone his leave or not, but I'm pretty sure had I been in his position, I would have done so – there's no way I was going to go on vacation while my soldiers invaded Samarra without me. First Lieutenant O'Brien, was a little miffed, too – the boss was leaving just as the big project was due, which left a lot of work on his plate. I could tell he was excited, though, as well – it's not often you get to command a cavalry troop in such a scenario.

When First Lieutenant O'Brien had finished his order, Sergeant First Class Martin and I headed back to his room to discuss the plan with Neathery and Barnes. I issued them a brief Warning Order covering the basics of the situation, our mission, and tomorrow's timeline, which they then passed on to the soldiers. With their help, I then drew up a working plan for the platoon, picking their brains to verify that we were covering all the bases and operating as soundly as possible. Then I headed back to my own room to write up the plan in full so I could brief it to the soldiers in the morning. Before I went to bed, I cleaned both my rifle and pistol, and emptied, cleaned, and then reloaded my magazines. I didn't sleep long, but I was able to sleep soundly despite my nerves. I knew I would need the rest – we would all have to be awake for the next 48 hours or more.

In the morning, before I gave my own platoon order, we met with Captain Black one more time to back-brief him on the mission, talking through our individual platoon plans and being quizzed on details and contingencies. There were no significant updates to the enemy situation from the previous night – estimates still ranged from 300 to 3,000 insurgents, with a core of experienced foreign fighters. They had almost certainly established defensive positions in key buildings, road blocks and barricades in the streets, and daisy-chained IEDs and booby-traps throughout the city.

My platoon formed up outside Sergeant First Class Martin's room, grabbing a seat on camp chairs or on the ground. I used a dry-erase marker to roughly sketch two large maps on the wall – one depicting the southeastern quadrant of Samarra, the other showing the whole city and the area to the east where our screen line would be established during the second phase of the operation.

"Gentlemen: Operation Baton Rouge." I gave them a second to

get their notebooks and pencils out, then launched into the detailed brief. It took just under an hour, but by quizzing them at the end, I could tell they had paid close attention. "Okay, you guys know what you have to take care of. I've got satellite imagery and digital maps with graphics for each Bradley commander, we're going to have a rehearsal this afternoon at 1500, then line up on the main road at 2130 for final inspection and checks."

The afternoon went by in a blur, as I juggled last minute details with my platoon and final meetings to receive intelligence and operational updates. Dinner at the chow hall that evening was somewhat surreal – the base had the unmistakable highly-charged atmosphere of a sports team before a championship game. Everyone had their own way of dealing with nerves or excitement – some were boisterously loud, others withdrawn and contemplative. For my part, I could hardly eat, and it wasn't just the soggy, bland food. I grabbed a couple granola bars and shoved them in my cargo pocket, in case my appetite returned later.

Out on the main road, my Bradleys were lined up last in Anvil Troop's vehicle line-up, since we would be on the southern flank of the assault. Walking back along the line of tracks, I ran into Bill Oberfeld, my opposite number in Anvil Troop, and shook his hand.

"Good luck, Bill."

"You too."

My Bradley commanders were already checking their soldiers when I got there, each man going over his crew's weapons and equipment with a practiced eye, quizzing the younger soldiers as he spot-checked.

"What's our mission?"

Private Richards pulled out his notepad and began reading our mission statement back to Staff Sergeant Neathery. I interrupted him.

"Richards: without the help of your notebook."

"Uh, I didn't memorize it, sir."

"That's okay, neither did I. What are we doing tonight?"

"We're going into Samarra, sir. We're attacking with Anvil Troop, then we hand things over to 2nd Brigade, and we set up a screen line."

"Right on," I told him.

Staff Sergeant Neathery handed Richards his weapon back, satisfied it was clean and fully functional. I continued down the line, pausing to quiz a few more soldiers, checking a first aid kit, asking to see extra batteries, or the meals and water we would need over the next three days, or the vehicle's latest maintenance report. I ended at Staff Sergeant Barnes' Bradley, where he had completed his checks and was lounging in his trademark reclined position on the Bradley's passenger bench, feet out on the back ramp.

"What's up, sir?" He asked, yawning.

"Not much," I said, mimicking his casually indifferent manner. "You guys all ready?"

Sergeant Zach Newsome, Barnes' gunner, snorted at my question. "Sheeeit. Are *you* ready, sir?"

"We'll see, huh, Zach?" I answered, smiling in the dim light from the Bradley's blue-green interior lights.

"Damn straight." He answered, taking a bite out of a bagel.

"As long as you got a good plan, that's all that matters," Staff Sergeant Barnes interjected, shifting on the bench to get more comfortable. "Like you, Zach. Your plan was to go to the chow hall and just bring back one bagel for yourself, and fuck the rest of us."

I laughed, and started heading back towards my own vehicle to set my gear in position.

"Hey, Red 1!" I stopped and back-tracked around to the rear of Sergeant First Class Martin's Brad, where he was seated on the step into the turret, a pair of radio handsets held to each ear.

"Mission's cancelled," he said, when I ducked in and squatted by him.

"You're fucking kidding," I said.

"Nope," he shook his head. "Stand down. Order just came from Anvil 6."

The order had technically come all the way down from the Iraqi Prime Minister, who had decided, for reasons unknown but probably political, that he didn't want U.S. forces going into Samarra just yet. Along the line in the dark, we swore in frustration and disappointment, not all of which was pretended. Though I was somewhat relieved, I would have preferred to have just gotten it over with, and all of us welcomed the chance to take the initiative for once and show the enemy how we could fight on *our* terms. As the soldiers took the vehicles back to the motor pool, I walked back to the rooms with Barnes and Martin. We were too keyed up to sleep, so we hung out for a while in Martin's room, making meaningless small talk about the mission and why it had been cancelled. Sergeant First Class Peterson from the mortars section dropped in later, and the conversation turned to women, as it often did.

"I'm gonna get me a sugar-mama when we get back," Barnes told us.

Martin was already laughing: "There you go again."

"No, I'm serious – a nice old broad, with tons of money. I'll give her two of my best years, and then I want *half!*"

"Aren't you married?" I reminded him, chuckling.

"Details, sir – that's just details."

"Ah," I said.

Barnes had his fantasy, and he was determined to run with it. "I'll be lying awake at night, feeling a little frisky, and I'll roll over and be like," he dropped to a whisper, *"Take your teeth out…"*

Peterson snorted. "You're not right, man. I dunno, I think the whole marriage thing is fucked up to begin with. I think marriage should be like enlistment contracts, you know? You sign up for three years, and then when your time's up, you say: 'Honey, we're in our reenlistment window, we gotta talk about what we want to do. Things are going pretty well, so we can sign up for another three years, or we can just do a six-month extension to think about it for a little more.'"

"You might be onto something there," I told him.

"Right? Think how low the divorce rate would be."

Eventually, the stresses of the day caught up to me, and I headed off to my own room to try to get a solid night's sleep.

CHAPTER EIGHT

"Hey, big guy: you got any weapons of mass destruction in there?"
-Red Platoon scout, pointing to the trunk of an Iraqi's car
while searching it at a checkpoint

The next morning we were told that Prime Minister Allawi had green-lit the mission to clear Samarra again, but that it was too late to go tonight, so everything had been pushed back until tomorrow. We were used to playing the waiting game, but we still hated being jerked around. So naturally, by mid-afternoon, Baton Rouge was back on for that night.

We had to scramble to get everything ready, but we made it – barely. As we were lining up, conducting final checks on the road just as we had the night before, two Airmen found me in the dark. They were both cameramen on an Air Force documentary team, assigned to cover the assault on Samarra from the front lines, and they wanted a ride to the action. Red 6 and I had the fewest dismounts on our tracks, so I gave him the photographer and crammed the videographer into the back of my Brad. I wasn't sure his experience level – what he'd seen and done in Iraq so far, in terms of enemy action.

"It's going to get hot," I warned him.

"Oh, I know – I've been in a Brad before. The engine heat makes it like a damn sauna," he said.

"No," I said, "I mean we're going to see some action – there's gonna be some serious shooting."

"That's good, sir! Makes for better videos."

"Okay, just so you know," I said.

This time there was no eleventh-hour cancellation – Operation Baton Rouge was on, and nothing in the world could stop it. At 10:30 p.m. on the 30th of September, we left the front gate with Anvil Troop, heading south towards Route Dover, the highway west to Samarra. We kept our lights on most of the way, but just before the city appeared over the horizon, we flipped off our headlights, the drivers switching on their night-vision periscopes and infrared headlights. The net was hushed, subdued, but my heart was pounding so loud I thought I could hear it over the roar of the diesel throbbing beneath me. It was a cool night, the summer's heat finally starting to abate.

As the city itself came into view, Bill Oberfeld's platoon peeled off the highway and headed north into the desert, the rest of the troop following him. The adrenaline was pumping through my veins now, a potent mix of fear and excitement; I took several deep breaths to calm myself, and tried to focus on my tasks ahead. We stopped when Staff Sergeant Barnes, in the trail Bradley, pulled several hundred yards off the road. Our vehicles then executed a 90° turn to the left, facing the city like a firing squad. We stayed there, hidden in the dark outside the city, and waited for the signal to attack. At midnight, Anvil 6 came on the net.

"Anvil, this is Anvil 6: start your movement."

It was a slow, deliberate movement, controlled with deadly calm. The troop was arrayed in a shallow vee formation running from north to south, the two tank platoons with Anvil 6 in the center leading slightly, Anvil Red Platoon in their Brads to the north, and my platoon to the south and slightly behind the tanks. We crested the final rise and the city unraveled before us, disconcertingly quiet and peaceful despite the situation. A shiver of anticipation ran down my spine.

The northern half of the troop reported small arms fire first, enemy tracers arcing out of the city towards the approaching vehicles. They returned fire immediately, Bradley gunners laying waste with 25mm fire, tank co-axial machine guns shredding off rounds into the night. I was momentarily distracted by the beauty of it – the brightly-glowing tracers zipping back and forth, criss-crossing the ground between us and the city. As I turned my attention back to the ground ahead of me and guiding my driver, a massive explosion rocked the earth ahead and to the right of us. *Mortars!*

I checked where the round had landed – it had not hit any friendly vehicles, but it had been close enough to rattle us.

"Red 1, Red 4."

"Yeah, I saw it," I replied.

"Roger: observed one round indirect fire, estimate 120mm mortar, grid: MC 982 874, over." Sergeant First Class Martin was as composed as ever, calmly rattling off the grid coordinate where the mortar had landed so I could report it on up the chain.

"Roger, out."

I jotted down the grid, checked it against my map, and grabbed the hand-mike for the troop radio. Anvil White was reporting an enemy dismount destroyed in their sector, and once they finished, I hopped in.

"Anvil 6, Bulldawg Red 1."

"Go ahead, Bulldawg."

"Roger." I passed on the mortar report, just as another round shattered into the ground ahead of us. They could clearly see us, and were getting closer with every round. "…just observed another round, stand by for location, over."

"Roger, I saw it, no need for location, over," Captain Black told me.

"Roger, out."

We continued closer to the city, the lumps of concrete coalescing into coherent buildings and streets, roofs and windows. When Captain Black judged we had approached close enough, we halted. At the southern edge of the battle, we were set at an odd angle to the city, and my gunner, Sergeant Wasser, let me know he couldn't see directly down the streets. I dropped down into the turret to see our sector through the gunsight. He was right – the city looked like one block of buildings from our angle, and we both knew that most of the enemy movement would be along the streets.

"We can't move," I told him, "It's too dangerous to clump together any closer with that mortar fire coming in."

As if to punctuate my warning, another round landed ahead of us. I stood back up in my turret hatch to see where it had hit. Farther up the line, an Anvil tank opened fire with the first main gun round of the fight, the flash momentarily whiting out my night vision goggles.

"Hell, yeah!" Schufeld yelled from the driver compartment.

"Wasser, concentrate your scanning on the rooftops if you can't see down the streets," I said. "I bet that's where their spotters are calling in the mortar fire from."

"Roger that," he replied. I saw the gun tube elevate and the turret began spinning slowly.

The mortars were only firing at us sporadically, but they were distressingly close – a single round landing on one of our vehicles could have killed that entire crew, armored plating or not. We needed air support, but only our lightly-armed Kiowas were on station so far, orbiting behind us, and I knew they were not likely to get permission to move over the city without ground forces below to support them – none of us wished to stage a *Blackhawk Down* reenactment this night. We would just have to gut it out and hope the mortars didn't find us first.

"Hey, sir?" It was one of my dismounts calling from the passenger compartment.

"Yeah, what's up?"

"The Air Force dude wants to get out and film stuff, sir."

I was slightly annoyed – he was just asking to do his job, but right now I had a platoon to command in combat, and I didn't want to have to worry about a Public Relations team as well.

"Negative – these mortar rounds are coming in too close, I don't want him running around outside the vehicle while there's so much shrapnel flying around."

"Roger."

"And tell him we might have to move again soon, so I don't want to have to wait for him to load up before we can displace."

"Roger."

I sat back down in the turret, set my night vision goggles aside, and pressed my face to the gunsight, watching the city as Wasser swung the turret back and forth across our sector, his eyes glued to his own gunsight. In contrast to the tank, which displays the thermal images in green, the Bradley sight is red-hued, which gives everything a menacing, sinister air. As we scanned, we picked up a hot spot – a splash of pink-white amidst the darker crimsons and blacks. Wasser centered the sight on the spot immediately.

"I got something," he said.

"I see it."

It was hard to see what the object was from our angle, but it looked like a man crouched in front of a wall. To our right, I heard the deep *thud-thud-thud* of a 25mm cannon. As we watched, the image onscreen vanished in a blur, hot clouds of fire and earth spraying around the man as the rounds impacted. One was a direct hit, chunks of gore spraying in all directions, splattering the wall behind him.

"Oh, man…" Wasser said.

"Fuck, that was nasty," I agreed. We could see pieces of the man stuck to the wall, still giving off heat in the infrared scope.

"Red 1, Red 6 – engaged and destroyed one enemy dismount with AK-47, over."

"Roger, nice shooting," I replied, and switched to the troop net to pass on the report.

"Sir, I think I got one!" Wasser told me.

"Where?" I put my face back onto the gunsight pads, peering into the viewer.

"Right there – see? On that rooftop?"

On a mid-sized building, a man was lying prone facing our direction.

"Yeah, roger – I see him." I squinted, trying to see him better. "Do you see a weapon?"

"Uh, I thought I did," Wasser answered, without much conviction.

I thought about it – by our rules of engagement, we were supposed to fire only at targets that were directly threatening us, but the rules tonight were murkier given the enemy situation – anyone in Samarra who wasn't hiding under their beds right now was looking for a fight. Regardless of whether the man had a weapon or not, he could easily have been serving as a spotter for the mortar team that was still lobbing rounds our way, so I decided that he was fair game.

"Can I shoot?" Wasser asked, clearly eager to record his first kill.

"Roger, engage."

I dimly heard Schufeld hooting with excitement down in his driver's station, but he was drowned out by the metallic din of the chain gun rattling into action as Wasser depressed the triggers. His first rounds landed slightly left, so he adjusted slightly, and put the second burst directly on target before the man had a chance to move.

"Nice," I told him. "I get to shoot next." I flipped to the troop radio. "Anvil 6, Bulldawg Red 1, engaged and destroyed one enemy dismount on rooftop, vicinity grid…" I rattled off the numbers, and added Red 6's earlier action report as well.

"This is Anvil 6, roger."

The troop was continuing to engage targets regularly up and down the line, the contact reports coming in a constant stream as more and more enemy appeared on the edge of the city for their chance to take a shot at us. It was a completely unfair fight: though they fired several RPGs at our positions, we had deliberately set our attack position outside their maximum range, while our weapons could easily reach out and touch anything we could see. I spent most of the time up in my hatch, scanning the city through my night vision goggles, and checking to make sure no enemy had snuck up on us on the ground.

"Switch out with me, sir?" Wasser asked. "My eyes are getting tired."

"Yeah, roger."

I hopped down again and sat, taking the controls and swinging the gun tube slowly back and forth across the city, stopping to check possible hot spots from time to time. It was hot down in the turret, and the sweat pooled where my forehead rested against the foam pad of the sight. I wiped my eyes and continued to scan. Suddenly, I saw a white blur in the sight. I flipped the magnification switch, zooming in on it.

"I think I got something," I announced, and heard Wasser drop down to his position next to me. My heart was pumping loudly.

"Another guy on a rooftop," Wasser noted, as I let the gun's glowing reticule rest on a hot spot partly obscured by a low wall. The spot ducked below the wall for a second, then came back up again, clearly a man looking in our direction, using the flat roof's perimeter wall as cover.

"Okay," I said, "Gun's hot? Just put the reticule on him and fire, right?"

"Yup," Wasser said. "Fire about a three or four round burst, we'll check your rounds, then adjust if necessary," he told me.

"Got it."

I thought, for a second, how completely absurd it was that my first time firing the Bradley would be in combat. I gripped the control handles firmly, feeling the massive turret respond smoothly to my touch as I eased the gun to the left a little, lining the insurgent up in the sight.

"On the way," I said.

The whole sight shook as the Bushmaster thundered out four rounds, the image blurring momentarily as the gun fired, and I watched the rounds arc through the picture, falling well short and destroying the corner of a hut a hundred meters short of the target.

"Shit," I said.

"Yeah. Your line's good, just bring it up. Eyeball it," Wasser told me.

I pulled back on the handles, hearing the hydraulics whine in response as the heavy barrel elevated. The reticule was several increments above the man now, who had ducked lower behind the short wall, but was still visible. I pulled the trigger again, bracing for the rounds this time.

"Target!" Wasser called out.

The rounds smashed into the wall in front of the enemy, blowing it apart and passing through into the man beyond. He disappeared in the cloud of exploding rounds, and we saw nothing of him again. I had killed a man.

It was strangely surreal for me – it's hard to feel one way or the other about such a momentous event when it's so impersonal, so detached and distant. It felt exactly like killing an enemy in a video game: there was no humanity to that white spot on my scope, no blood or agony to acknowledge having caused, just the simple fact that he was no longer there. I had expected to feel changed somehow by the experience, but nothing seemed different. I felt like I should feel sorry somehow – *had he really been threatening us? Was I right to kill him? Had he died immediately, or suffered horribly?* I felt slightly guilty that it had been so easy and so disproportionately unsporting of a fight.

I had little time to reflect on it further, as the battle progressed quickly after my kill. As I stood back up in my hatch to get a better picture of the tactical situation, a mortar round crashed into the earth about 75 meters from our vehicle, the impact rattling the whole vehicle.

"Holy shit!"

"Yeah, that was too close." I sent the report to Anvil 6, pointing out that the rounds were getting closer to my platoon's locations.

Technically, we don't report that over the net – *if* the enemy has managed to get hold of a U.S. radio, *if* he has the proper decryption key and knows how to code it in, and *if* he's figured out what channel we're broadcasting on and is monitoring our radio traffic, he could theoretically adjust his aim if we reported the incoming rounds' location relative to our own. But that's a lot of really big "ifs" – if we were fighting the Russians in World War Three, it might have been a possibility, but Iraqi insurgents? Not so much. Anvil 6 didn't call me on my faux pas.

"Roger, Bulldawg Red 1. All Anvil elements: Squadron has received control of a Specter gunship coming on station, and is passing control to me."

The AC-130 Specter gunship is a modified version of the standard C-130 cargo plane; instead of an empty cargo hold, the AC-130 is equipped with a variety of heavy weapons, which, depending on the specific variant, can include a 25mm Gatling gun, a 40mm cannon, and a 105mm light artillery piece. All of these weapons are tied in to a sophisticated thermal video camera, which allows them to target individual enemy soldiers and vehicles with pinpoint accuracy from several thousand feet in the air.

We could hear the aircraft circling above us, the drone of its heavy propeller engines distinct over the background noise of the battle, but we could not see it. The Kiowa team in our sector, which had been working their way up and down the edge of the city looking for targets of opportunity, pulled back away from the city, banking hard and fast to clear the impact area. The enemy mortar team was the first to go, the spotters in the aircraft quickly locating them from above. With shocking force, a 105mm shell crashed into the inner city, lighting up the night as it detonated, showering sparks and flame everywhere. Three more shells followed right behind it in quick succession: *BOOM-BOOM-BOOM!* We whooped and cheered from our hatches, awestruck at the demonstration. The Specter shifted targets rapidly, smearing first one enemy position and then another, often firing with multiple weapons systems at the same time. It was like watching someone use a sledgehammer to squash cockroaches – total overkill. I turned to Wasser, who had given up scanning to come out of his hatch and watch the fireworks show.

"Jesus," I said.

"That thing is fucking *bad*," he agreed.

I nodded, wide-eyed: "I think if God ever smote someone, he would use Specter."

After several minutes of gleeful hunting, the gunship ran out of targets, the rattled and dazed enemy survivors going to ground to escape the menace above. Under the new threat, the enemy stopped firing at us, too, so in order to maintain enemy contact, Anvil 6 decided to press forward with his tanks. The Bradleys – whose thinner armor made them more vulnerable to mines, IEDs, and RPGs – would remain in place, covering the tanks' movement, and move forward when the tanks had cleared the area of larger threats.

Staff Sergeant Neathery was in my northernmost Bradley, and was monitoring the platoon internal net of Anvil Green, the tank platoon next to him. He watched as the tanks moved forward of his position, approaching the buildings cautiously, turrets scanning fast. Anvil Green 4 was the closest tank to his position, and as he watched, the tank rolled past what looked like a bomb crater or some other large hole in the ground. Suddenly, two men stood up in the hole – they had been lying flat in the hole and had managed to remain hidden while the tank passed. One of them shouldered an RPG, pointing it at the rear deck of the tank.

Neathery had no time to warn Anvil Green 4 – he grabbed his Bradley's control handles and fired a sustained burst into the hole, with the tank still just feet away. The RPG team vanished in a burst of exploding shells. The tank screeched to a halt.

"Woah! What the fuck, Bulldawg Red?!"

Thinking the rounds had been fired in error, Anvil Green 4 was justifiably pissed, and was getting ready to chew some ass when he took a look in the hole and saw what was left of the RPG team.

"Hey, ignore my last – thanks, Red 5, owe ya one."

"Roger, that – we're here for you."

Even with the Spectre gunship still on station, the tanks regained contact easily, sparking up several close-quarters gun battles with insurgents on the streets and in buildings. As their machine guns dealt out death to the enemy close in, the gunship above destroyed any enemy forces foolish enough to try to move to the tanks' location to reinforce their comrades. On one occasion, the gunship even cleared "danger close" fires with Anvil 6, the tankers buttoning up in their hatches as the Air Force gunners poured a ring of fiery steel onto targets surrounding the tanks at close range.

The tanks in the city took some pretty heavy contact – several were hit by RPG rounds, which glanced harmlessly off their armor, detonating ineffectively or ricocheting into a nearby building. They fired their main guns several times, destroying dug-in enemy positions in buildings and street barricades. But after half an hour of stirring up trouble within the objective area with the tanks, contact began to wane, and Anvil 6 made the call to withdraw. At around 3 a.m., the tanks left the city, rejoining us in our attack position while we waited for the elements of 2nd Brigade to arrive to conduct the passage of lines and take over the area. By 4 a.m. they had showed up on the highway to the south, and the ground commander contacted Anvil 6 to initiate the passage of lines. For whatever reason, perhaps because I was closest, Captain Black decided to delegate the linkup duties to me, so as Anvil Troop prepared to move back to FOB Mackenzie, I located their commander's Humvee section and hopped down from my Brad with my map.

"Are you Captain Black?" He asked, as I walked up.

"No, sir – Lieutenant Platt. Captain Black sent me, though."

"Okay," he said, shaking my hand, "Watkins, from 1-77 Armor. What's happened so far?"

"A lot," I told him, grinning as I spread my map on the hood of his truck. I gave him a brief summary of our operation, detailing the types of contact we had observed and their rough locations.

"Are there more in there, you think?"

I nodded. "Probably. I'm sure we didn't get them all, but we put a big hurt on them, and they're definitely not going to be able to organize as stiff a resistance as they could have before. I don't think they'll be able to organize much of anything, anymore."

"Good," he said. "Thanks."

"Good luck, sir," I said, and meant it. We might have taken the brunt of the enemy contact of Operation Baton Rouge, but this next phase would still be extremely dangerous, tedious, and exhausting. Now that the adrenaline rush was wearing off and my fatigue was setting in heavily, I was glad to have the worst behind us. I headed back to my track, climbed up into my hatch, and picked up my hand mike.

"Anvil 6, Bulldawg Red 1."

"This is Anvil 5, 6 is on the ground, over."

"Roger, Anvil 5: briefing of 1-77 complete. Since we're at the next phase of the operation, I'd like to switch to Bulldawg Troop control and move to my traffic control point position, over."

"This is Anvil 5, roger: execute. I'll advise Anvil 6."

"Bulldawg Red 1, roger, out."

Wasser had heard the conversation and was already tweaking the radio knobs, switching me to the Bulldawg Troop frequency. I reminded the rest of the platoon to do the same, then gave a radio check on the Bulldawg Troop frequency.

Sergeant First Class Peterson, who was manning the improvised troop command post at the retrans site, answered.

"This is Bulldawg X-Ray, roger – good to have you back, Red 1."

"Roger, X-Ray – good to be back."

After a short drive, we stopped at the predetermined location, and keeping four of my Bradleys zig-zagged across the road to act as a blocking position, I sent Staff Sergeant Barnes north to link up with Blue Platoon's Bradleys, who were already set in a screen line stretching north to south. While they picked their positions and ensured that the off-road section of the screen line was without gaps, we set up razor wire across the road and hung chemical lights off it to make it visible to drivers in the pre-dawn darkness. Bill Oberfeld's platoon was responsible for the terrain south of my roadblock, between the road and the Tigris, and I checked in with him early on to coordinate between our platoons, just as we had with Blue Platoon to the north, to ensure we had an unbroken line of vehicles cordoning off the entire city.

By dawn we were set, and the sun rose on a dramatic scene that morning. The roofs of Samarra were visible in the distance, and the night's fighting had started several massive fires, grey-black plumes of smoke rising in thick columns over the city. We didn't hear any evidence of ongoing battle, however – as it turned out, we saw all of the intense combat of the operation, and though the clearing of the city would continue for several days while we manned our screen line, the units in the city went about their business with only sporadic enemy contact. They turned up a prolific amount of weapons and ammunition, all of which was driven to the perimeter of the city and destroyed in several spectacular controlled demolitions. But they didn't catch any of the high priority targets – as they had before, when faced with a full-scale clearing operation, the insurgents merely tossed away their weapons and blended into the population, waiting to fight another day.

At the time, we thought of the mission as a historic and overwhelming success: my platoon alone killed more than 20 insurgents during the night, and across the city, between ground forces and air strikes the full tally was estimated at 150 or more killed, with no coalition casualties. That was a good night's work in anyone's book, and we were proud of our contribution regardless of the clearing operation's outcome. It's hard to get a feeling for how the people of Samarra felt (especially when you're holding a rifle while asking them); on the whole, the ones we talked to later that day at our checkpoint were pretty enthusiastic about the operation – much as with the Taliban in Afghanistan, life under insurgent rule had not been all sunshine and rainbows. In addition to forcing their radical Islamist values on the mainly Sunni population (banning TV, music, and dancing, among other things), the insurgents in Samarra had made it a practice to take what they wanted without asking, up to and including houses and women.

Not long after dawn, the cars began arriving at our checkpoint. Samarra is a relatively large city of several hundred thousand people, and besides hosting a major battle that night, the citizens discovered several thousand troops still in the city at daybreak, industriously kicking down doors and tossing rooms. This had naturally given the locals plenty of incentive to leave town for the weekend.

My orders were clear, however: no military age males could leave or enter the city. This is standard operating procedure on such a mission – we needed to prevent insurgents from escaping, and prevent more insurgents from entering the city to attack friendly forces from areas they had already cleared. The reality of selectively sealing off the city, however, was in stark contrast to the simplicity of our mission statement. One at a time, we would let a car into the search area, thoroughly check it for contraband, turn the males back towards Samarra, and let the females and children continue. By 9 a.m. we had at least 200 cars stacked up outside our roadblock, stretching most of the way back to Samarra. With only 15 soldiers at the checkpoint, it was going to be a long day of searching.

As the morning progressed, however, the cars continued to stack up, until we lost sight of the end of the line. Out of concern that insurgents might sneak either a car bomb or a sniper team out to target us from one of the cars, Staff Sergeant Neathery asked to take a team outside our blocking position to patrol along the line of cars. They returned 15 or 20 minutes later looking shaken. Neathery found me quickly.

"It's bad out there, sir."

"How so?"

"Well, for starters, the line goes way back. We're not going to get to even a quarter of those cars today."

I nodded: that was unfortunate, but there wasn't much we could do about it.

"But there's a lot of people hurt, too – I saw a woman with a gunshot wound in the back, and a kid with some bad shrapnel wounds."

I frowned. "Why aren't they going to the hospital in Samarra?"

"I don't know, sir."

Martin wandered up, having overheard some of Neathery's concerns. Between the three of us, we worked out a plan to triage the cars in line, using Neathery's advance team to move the wounded to the front of the line. Under my orders, we sped up our search process on those cars carrying injured civilians, too – I was willing to accept a bit more risk to get them on their way faster. I found our platoon's interpreter, a hard-working Iraqi named Mohammed, as the first cars of wounded people began arriving.

"Mohammed!"

"Yes?"

I gestured to a woman standing by her car as it was searched, her young son's arm bandaged heavily. "Can you ask this woman why they are leaving the city – why didn't she go to the hospital in Samarra?"

He echoed my words. She shook her head, fear in her eyes, and replied quietly, avoiding eye contact with me.

"She says the fighters have taken over the hospital – they made everyone leave," Mohammed told me.

"American fighters?"

He relayed my question. She shook her head – no. I swore.

"That's fucked up," Sergeant First Class Martin, standing next to me, agreed.

In addition to Mohammed, our platoon had two medics assigned to us for the mission, in recognition of the danger of manning such a checkpoint. Though their main job was to treat us if anything happened, Sergeant Chambers had been helping out the search teams as the cars moved through the checkpoint, but as the wounded began to arrive, he jogged over to me and asked permission to treat those he could.

"Yeah, you bet, Doc. Do you have enough supplies?"

"For now, sir, but if we keep getting people through at this rate..." he left the sentence unfinished.

"Okay, I'll see what I can do to get some more out here. Keep an eye on your supplies, and make sure you have some set aside in case we take contact."

"Roger – I can't treat 'em all, sir." It was clear that he would have liked to.

"Okay," I told him. "Do what you can."

The day dragged on, a seemingly endless train of human suffering passing by our eyes under the hot sun. We searched so many cars that it all became a giant blur. We actually kept count, and though I've forgotten the exact figure, it was close to five hundred that day alone.

We saw families crying as we split them, husbands sending their wives and children on alone, and turning away to walk back to Samarra on foot. There was a ten-year-old boy grinning as he drove his father's old Mercedes through the checkpoint, standing on the floor to be able to see over the wheel, his mother and sisters modestly covering their faces as they passed my soldiers. Another car held a boy with a chemical burn on his arm, who didn't make a sound as Doc Chambers wrapped his arm in gauze and gave his grandmother a small bottle of ointment for him. By evening, we had all been awake for close to 40 hours straight, during which time we had fought in the longest and most dangerous battle of our tour in Iraq, and then spent a long, sweaty day manning the checkpoint.

Blue Platoon scored the first and only success of the screen line. As they took their positions, they spotted a red pickup truck moving towards them off-road at high speed. When the driver disregarded their signals to stop, they fired a warning shot, which had the intended effect. A very rattled 14-year-old boy was at the wheel, and after patting him down, they were about to let him go with a stern warning when one of the dismounted scouts flipped the tarp off the back of his truck for a quick peek. He found a veritable arms bazaar underneath: grenades of every type imaginable, RPG launchers, AK-

47s, the whole shebang. When they laid all the weapons out for inventory, they took up over 50 square feet of ground.

After sunset, we had Mohammed tell the cars remaining in line that they would have to come back the following day – our orders were to close the checkpoint at night. Once the line of cars had cleared the area and full dark had set in, we let out a collective sigh of relief. The effects of sleep deprivation were starting to show heavily in all of us – slurred speech, slow reactions and thought processes; it was like being fairly drunk, with none of the buzz. I should have been hungry, but was literally too tired to eat – my body was overriding the hunger mechanism in favor of rest. I worked out the guard rotation for the night with my crew and then crashed.

*   *   *

The original operational plan called for us to man the checkpoint for three days, but we ended up manning that screen line for *nine*. 2nd Brigade took longer than expected to clear Samarra fully, but after they finished, 1st Infantry Division decided to maintain the screen line, presumably to deter insurgents from returning. Nine days straight is a long time to do anything, but if those nine days include prolonged activity in 100° heat, not showering, and only having a few days' worth of clothing, things start to get ugly. Or rather, smell ugly. We had baby wipes, which we used both as toilet paper and as a way to clean ourselves, but they can only do so much.

As a result of living in such close proximity with limited hygiene options, almost all of us got sick quickly. I came down with a nasty cold, which made life pretty miserable in the afternoon heat, but I downed Tylenol and kept myself hydrated and got over it in a couple days. Sergeant First Class Martin's gunner, Sergeant Tremont, had it worse, catching a nasty stomach virus which hit him with the dreaded one-two punch of diarrhea and vomiting. He refused treatment for a while, stoically manning his position on the checkpoint, hurrying off into the bushes to do his business when necessary, until Sergeant First Class Martin had had enough and ordered him over to the medics. They gave him three IV bags full of fluid, and we put him on the next convoy back to FOB Mackenzie to get full treatment. He was right back out on the checkpoint as soon as he was cleared for duty by the Squadron Medical Officer.

They brought us out hot food, occasionally, and managed to bring out some of our spare clothes when the situation got dire enough. Given the number of nicotine addicts in our troop, dwindling tobacco supplies quickly became the biggest problem, however. One night, as Sergeant First Class Peterson was collecting the platoon sergeants' resupply requests over the radio, it became clear that each platoon was getting down to its last cigarette and pinch of dip – he had spent five minutes compiling the list of food and water requests, and a solid 20 minutes writing down tobacco products requested.

"Okay," Peterson said, "I've got the list here, but I just want to let you guys know that I don't think anyone is planning on making another re-supply run for another couple days."

There followed several curse-laden transmissions from the platoons. A pair of Kiowas from Eagle Troop happened to be giving our screen line air support that night, and they were listening in on our troop net so that they could coordinate tactically with us if needed.

"Bulldawg X-Ray, Eagle 19."

"Eagle 19, this is X-Ray."

"Roger, I've been monitoring your net about the tobacco requests – got an idea. If you have someone meet me at the landing pad back at Mackenzie on our next trip back to refuel, we can drop that stuff off at your location when we return to sector."

"Eagle 19, Bulldawg X-Ray: I think that would be extremely appreciated, over."

"Well, Eagle 19 has been there himself."

We got a huge kick out of it – a special airlift of smokes.

One of the small blessings about the whole operation was that First Lieutenant O'Brien was in charge still, with Captain Hoffman on leave, and since O'Brien trusted Sergeant First Class Peterson and First Lieutenant Thomas implicitly and was often called away for staff meetings, the two of them largely ran the troop themselves from the temporary command post out at FOB Rex. Peterson knew just how bored we all were in the evenings – the checkpoints were closed, our DVD and mp3 players were out of batteries, and we had nothing to do but sit around in the dark. One evening, he decided to hold a talk-show over the tactical net, reading us a "bedtime story" out of *Penthouse,* complete with background sound effects added by First Lieutenant Thomas. It was wildly popular, and the following day, he was back by overwhelming popular demand.

That afternoon, Peterson gave himself a quick "plug" in between tactical reports: "Jim and I had been happily married for four years, and on our fifth anniversary he decided to give me something special. He knew I'd always wanted to try a threesome...these stories and more, coming to you live at 2230, courtesy of *Penthouse Forum* letters and your friendly operations center crew."

Later that evening, while Peterson was reading us the final *Penthouse* story of the night, a pair of Darkhorse Troop helicopters checked in over the net, interrupting the story to let us know they were on station. After they finished their check-in report, Peterson acknowledged, and then remained silent. I figured he must have finished for the night, but one of the section sergeants over in Blue Platoon wasn't satisfied.

"X-Ray, Blue 5. Are you gonna continue the story, or should we just go to sleep?"

"Blue 5, this is X-Ray, roger...I really don't think Darkhorse 32 wants to hear the rest of the story."

Darkhorse 32 was quick to jump in: "Hey, uh, X-Ray...we'd like to know what happens."

"...so does Darkhorse 5," the other aircraft added.

"Oh...well, okay then." He cleared his throat. "We now return to the conclusion of our story, here on Love Phones at Night on 99.3 KVHL: 'Cav Hell.' When we left off, Vanessa had gone in for a sensual massage with Rick..."

The bedtime stories got so famous, the Kiowa pilots were known to have rearranged their flight schedule to ensure they were within our airspace at the proper time each night. Some nights, just to shake things up, the show took callers:

"This is Dr. Love, here to answer all your pressing questions...let's take another call. This one's from Mike, in Utica. What's up, Mike?"

Over in his track, I heard Staff Sergeant Barnes key the net.

"Hey, Dr. Love – longtime listener, first-time caller, I just love your show, over."

"Well, thanks, Mike," Peterson replied. "What can I help you with?"

"Well, Dr. Love, I've got this, problem, see. My wife's 6 months pregnant, but I've been in Iraq for the last 9 months. Do you think I should be worried?"

The radio nets in general provided a great deal of amusement to us all, throughout the rotation. Everything is funnier when broadcast over a tactical net for some reason, perhaps because we place so much emphasis on net discipline and concise, accurate reports. Peterson in particular loved using the nets for social purposes when his convoys passed other friendly units:

"Hey, shout out to my man P-Squared, looking sexy out there, looking good!"

Everyone would turn up their radios when it sounded like someone was about to get in trouble with headquarters, just to snicker as the drama played out over the airwaves. During one stint at FOB Rex back with my tank platoon, I had forgotten to bring some maintenance equipment out with me to test the quality of our engine oil, and as a result, First Lieutenant O'Brien had gotten in hot water with Squadron headquarters for missing an important deadline. He called me up that evening, but skirted around the issue for a few minutes, asking pointed questions.

"Green 1, Bulldawg 5: do you remember when I told you to bring that equipment out to the Retrans site yesterday?"

"This is Green 1, roger."

"And you do realize how important tank maintenance is, Green 1?"

It was entirely my fault, but I felt like he was patronizing me, so, like a wise-ass, I suggested he just get the ass-chewing over with, since there was nothing either of us could do about the issue at that point. He obliged, and let me have it for a while, finishing with a threat to fire me:

"...and if you can't meet basic mission requirements, Lieutenant, I'll send someone else out there who can!"

Staff Sergeant Peiper, clearly enjoying the rant, quickly chimed in: "When he comes out, can you tell the new guy to bring that maintenance equipment we forgot?"

*   *   *

On the checkpoint outside Samarra, our orders changed soon after 2nd Brigade finished clearing the city: military age males were now permitted to pass through the checkpoint, in addition to women and children. To ensure no insurgents were entering or exiting the city, we started checking every man's name, with Mohammed's help, against a BOLO (Be On the Look Out) list of known insurgents provided by Division. This list was without photos, however, so it was child's play for any insurgent to get through the checkpoint without being caught – they just had to say they had no ID, and give a false name. It was a poor system, to be sure, but I suppose it was better than nothing – we did catch one man whose name was on the list, and detained him before sending him on for processing back at Mackenzie.

We had a fair amount of people pass through the checkpoint on foot – for security's sake, we didn't let them just wander through unescorted; once we had a small group of them together, one soldier would take them through the position to the far side. Back from his bout with the flu, Sergeant Tremont drew this duty one day, and I had to laugh as I noticed that he was marching a group of five Iraqi men across the checkpoint, *calling cadence.*

"Hey la-dee-dah-day! [pause for response] Hey la-dee-dah-dee-ay! I used to wear blue jeans! Now I'm wearing Army greens!"

The Iraqis figured it out, of course, and started to laugh and play along, goose-stepping in time to his singing. About our only significant find of the mission came from the trunk of a Baghdad University psychology professor's car. He raised suspicions by having a ton of CDs in his car, which was unusual for Iraq – not many people there own a PC, though we had noticed internet cafes starting to spring up in larger towns. We popped a CD into Sergeant First Class Martin's laptop to see what it contained, but the disc drive wouldn't read it.

"Maybe it's a DVD?" I asked.

"Hold on," Barnes told me. He returned a few seconds later with his portable DVD player. I popped the disc in, the screen flickered on, and we were greeted by a grainy video showing two men enjoying a woman.

"Woah!"

"Hey, guys, check this out!"

Things slowed down for a bit on the checkpoint, as more of the soldiers drifted toward the commotion. I had to laugh as I watched the guys work their way through half a dozen DVDs, looking for the better quality stuff. They ended up buying most of the guy's collection, who thought this was all pretty funny. Eventually Neathery wandered over from the front entrance to the checkpoint, clearly annoyed that everyone had abandoned their positions, although there were no cars in sight at the time.

"What the hell are you guys doing?" He asked.

"Uh...verifying contraband," someone piped up. The professor spoke up then, in broken English.

"You want see good movie?"

"Yeah, man," Barnes told him. "Break out the good shit."

The older man sifted through his stack for a bit, then pulled out a disc, which they eagerly loaded up. The video quality was terrible, so it took us a couple seconds to make it out, and we were sorry we did: it prominently featured a hermaphrodite.

There was a chorus of loud groans.

"Aw, dude!"

"Shit! Turn it off!"

The doctor was confused – he genuinely thought this was the cream of his crop. It wasn't our last run-in with sexual deviance in Iraq: while conducting a routine air patrol one night, two Darkhorse Kiowas caught a local farmer working over one of his sheep in the middle of a field. They even managed to snap some thermal video footage of the act before the man heard them and ran off. To be fair, I'm sure that if you flew missions all over rural America for a year, you'd probably come across someone doing the same thing.

Mohammed the interpreter got a huge kick out of the fact that we bought the man's porn collection, and stood there laughing as the money was exchanged.

"What are you laughing at, Mohammed?" Staff Sergeant Barnes asked him.

"Naughty, naughty!" He said, and shook his head patronizingly.

"I don't know why you're on your high horse, Mohammed," I told him. "You're the 45-year-old who's working as an interpreter so he can afford a new 18-year-old wife."

"16 years old," he corrected me, grinning broadly. "And it's expensive to have three wives."

*   *   *

On our ninth consecutive day manning the checkpoint, we finally got orders to pack it up and head back to FOB Mackenzie. I've never seen soldiers break down a checkpoint so quickly or enthusiastically: grins a mile wide, we policed up the last of our trash and loaded everyone into the Bradleys. Just feeling the rushing wind of driving again was a welcome change, and though we stayed alert as we moved back, everyone's mind was on a well-deserved shower and a full night's uninterrupted sleep on a luxurious cot. As we pulled in on the main road of FOB Mackenzie, we stopped briefly and I jumped out to check in at the troop operations center to see how long we had to recover.

"24 hours," First Lieutenant O'Brien informed me. "Division has decided to maintain that checkpoint indefinitely, so you guys get to go do it all over again."

"Roger," I said tiredly, "I'm going to go check email."

"Oh," he said, "You guys haven't heard? Squadron shut down the internet café – an Anvil trooper had their rifle stolen while they were checking email."

"Stolen…by who?" I said. "That's absurd."

"I know. The rumor is it fell off their tank while they were out on mission, and he just came up with the internet café story to cover his ass. Anyway, café is closed until further notice, I believe the official statement was: 'If you have time to check email, you have time to go out and help try to find the missing weapon.'"

I shook my head in disgust. "Yeah, I'll get right on that."

I knew my fiancée would be worried about me – it had been nine days since we had last spoke. I left the troop bunker and crunched across the gravel to the phone trailer next door. There was a note taped to the door: "Phones down – satellite uplink broken. Part on order from States." I was about to start looking for a carrier pigeon, when I realized official email should still be working, so I begged my way onto First Lieutenant O'Brien's work computer and sent off a quick note to everyone letting them know I was okay.

Next I headed to the motor pool to give the guys an update on our mission for the following day. Recovery operations were proceeding well on the vehicles, the men sweating in the afternoon heat as they checked fluid levels, reloaded ammunition boxes, and replaced broken parts on the vehicles. We cleaned our weapons in the afternoon, switched out batteries on our flashlights and night-vision goggles, and dropped our laundry off at the laundry site. I had a bunch of care packages waiting for me, which I opened and dropped by my soldiers' rooms for them to rifle through. Finally, after dinner, we had a chance to relax for a few hours – it would be an early start in the morning.

Relishing the moment, I peeled off my combat gear and headed to the showers in my flip-flops and flak vest, stumbling tiredly in the rocks and sand before climbing the stairs to the well-lit trailer. It was strangely empty, which I failed to notice, hanging up my towel and stripping before turning on the water. The water dribbled out in a lazy gurgle from the bottom of the showerhead – our water purification unit was busted. It was a poetic ending to the day, but the humor was entirely lost on me as I stood under the gentle drip and tried to wash the grime of nine days off. At least my cot wasn't broken.

CHAPTER NINE

"I flew through Dallas on R&R Leave, and it was crazy, man.
There were people everywhere cheering and yelling, hugging
everyone. This little girl ran right up to me, so I picked her up and
planted a kiss on that little fucker, and then I guess she realized I
wasn't her daddy, and she looked a little scared. Her mom thought it
was funny, though."
-*Lieutenant Joey Thomas*

I was finishing a crossword in my room one afternoon a few weeks
later, killing time between patrols and chatting with my roommate,
Brian Pierce, when Dave Williams banged on our door. Dave was a
Kiowa pilot in Darkhorse Troop who had arrived at Squadron at the
same time I had, so we had become good friends during in-
processing back in Germany.

"Okay, boys," he said. "Flip for it! Who wants to ride a Kiowa?"

Brian had to man a shift in the operations center in an hour, but I
was all for it, so I grabbed my gear and Dave and I hopped in his
Humvee, heading for the air troop bunkers. Kiowas break down
from time to time, and once repairs are completed, they have to be
taken up for a rigorous test flight by a pilot certified as a maintenance
tester before they can be cleared for missions. Kiowas are small
aircraft designed for scouting, so they don't carry passengers – just a
pilot and co-pilot. Maintenance test flights are usually done by a lone

pilot, but that leaves an open seat in the cockpit, so it's the only time a "passenger" can see what riding in a Kiowa is like. Unfortunately, it's also the most dangerous time, since the helicopter was in pieces a few hours prior. Still, I wasn't going to miss my opportunity to take a ride.

At the hangars, Dave suited me up in his flight vest and helmet before taking me out to the flight pad to meet Chief Beauregard, the test pilot. Beauregard was giving the bird a thorough visual inspection, but when he saw us walking up, he stopped and pointed into the open engine maintenance hatch, addressing Dave.

"Hey, what does this thing do?"

I laughed, and we shook hands.

"Okay, sir," he told me. "Obviously, don't touch anything inside the cockpit I don't ask you to touch. I'm going to hand you the flight checklist so you can read it to me while I do the tests."

"Got it," I said.

"Other than that, sit back and enjoy the ride," he grinned.

"...and don't puke," Dave added.

"Shouldn't you be getting your crew rest?" I shot back.

By regulation, pilots must have a certain amount of rest time between flights to ensure that they are fully alert and capable for each mission, called "crew rest." Those of us who enjoyed no such mandatory down-time privileges liked to call it their "beauty sleep."

Beauregard and I climbed aboard, and Dave pointed out some of the cockpit controls to me while the Chief got settled. I noticed that this aircraft had its cockpit doors installed, for which I was secretly grateful: most Kiowa crews take the cockpit doors off for better visibility and to allow them to fire their rifles at ground targets.

"This is the stick," Dave explained, jostling the joystick between my knees. "In addition to 'steering' the aircraft, the stick lets you control all of the targeting and weapons systems with these buttons." I watched the green computer display in front of me as Dave flicked a few switches and buttons, expertly scrolling through menus and controlling the Mast-Mounted Sight, a bulbous ball mounted directly above the rotors, which contained sophisticated thermal imaging and laser designation systems.

"On the left side, here, is your throttle – which you twist just like on a motorcycle. You always fly with one hand on the stick, and the other on the throttle, and then your feet work those two pedals to control yaw."

"Yaw?"

"So you can turn while hovering, or keep the aircraft in 'trim' while flying – that way the nose stays aligned with the tail, it keeps everything aerodynamic."

I whistled. "Complex."

"Yeah," he said, "But when you've flown enough, it all gets to be second nature."

"So the guy in the left seat is helping to fly?" I asked.

"No," Dave corrected me, "not usually. They'll switch out during missions, but it would be too difficult for the two pilots to cooperate that closely to fly the bird at the same time. The 'left-seater' handles the tactical stuff – weapons, the Mast-Mounted Sight, radio reporting, coordinating with ground units, etc."

"Ah – gotcha."

"While you're up there, keep an eye out for birds," Dave advised.

"Birds? Like crows, sea gulls?" I asked.

"Yeah. We've got a competition going in the air troops to see who can kill the most," he told me. "It started as an accident, someone hit one and we all laughed about it, but guys are starting to take it pretty seriously now – we've got a whiteboard up in the bunker listing kills right now."

I laughed. "Doesn't that fuck up the Kiowa at all?"

"Yeah, actually – it can jack up the airframe pretty bad. It's kind of like Russian roulette, now that I think about it."

"Okay," Chief Beauregard said, looking up from his station as he buckled himself in, "Let's do this."

"Have fun!" Dave told me, punching my shoulder.

"I will," I said, grinning.

We started with the pre-flight checklist, which ended with lighting the engine. As the rotors reached full speed, Chief Beauregard scratched his chin and played with a few switches, throttling the engine up and down a few times.

"Hmmmm," he said, in a contemplative, less-than-reassuring way. "I think they put the rotors on wrong."

I figured he was messing with me again.

"Well, maybe 'wrong' is kind of a bad way of putting it," he told me, his voice sounding tinny over the noise-reducing intercom system. "There are two ways of putting them on, and I don't think they did it the best way."

I was beginning to realize how utterly stupid it had been for me to have gotten into a *recently broken* helicopter. I said, "Is that it, then?"

"Naw," he shook his head. "We can still fly. It's just a little pet peeve of mine. What's next on the checklist?"

"Hover tests," I told him, after consulting the book.

"Okay," he craned his neck to see all around the aircraft, then throttled up again, the bird rising about ten feet in the air under his deft control. "We're gonna want a little more room."

We scooted across the hangar area, setting down a couple hundred yards away on the main runway of the FOB. First we did a straight hover test, rising six feet up and remaining in place for several seconds. Next, Chief Beauregard slid the bird forwards, backwards, and side-to-side, checking that the aircraft responded correctly to his commands in each case. Finally, we spun in a slow circle, rotating the chopper around the axis of its rotor.

"Okay, everything working fine there – let's have a little fun." Before I could respond, Beauregard gave the engine full throttle, pushing the aircraft to about 80 mph as we tore down the runway a mere eight feet off the ground. As we neared the end of the runway, he pulled back on the stick, and the scout helicopter responded immediately, roaring into a steep climb that made me grunt out loud from the g-forces.

As we gained height, Chief Beauregard pushed the stick over, banking hard right until the bird was practically on its side. I let out a "whoo!" from the sheer excitement of it. Beauregard chuckled.

"Best roller coaster you'll ever ride, sir."

"I can't argue with that!"

As he leveled the aircraft, we heard a pair of Kiowas check in with Darkhorse X-Ray over the net, requesting permission to take off and use the test fire range.

"Oh, good deal," the Chief told me, "We'll ride with them when they do their test runs so you can see a little gunnery."

As we wheeled in a wide circle, I watched as the two birds lifted off from the pad below us and made their way towards the test-fire range, a collection of several burned-out Iraqi armored vehicles north of the FOB. Chief Beauregard dropped in behind the two aircraft as they approached the range, alerting us that they were going "weapons hot." Kiowas aim their .50 caliber machine gun by pointing the entire aircraft at the target, and the aircraft is so light that the .50 cal shakes the whole airframe when it fires.

Both Kiowas made excellent back-to-back runs, raining tracers down onto the armored hulks before peeling off for a quick rearm prior to their mission. Not to be outdone, Chief Beauregard decided he would test fire our own .50 cal, and he pushed us into a shallow dive. He pulled the trigger on his stick, and the .50 cal beside me roared into action, thumping out a 15-round burst that landed short initially, but Beauregard expertly walked the rounds forward and onto the target, tracers ricocheting off the steel plating.

Before we "overflew" the target, Chief Beauregard threw us into a tight bank, juking through a complex series of maneuvers which made my stomach flip several times. Somehow, we ended up at altitude again and pointed back toward the target, though I couldn't for the life of me remember how.

"That's what we call the 'Return to Target' maneuver," Beauregard told me.

"Nice," I lied, trying to regain some of my equilibrium.

We continued through a few more checks back on the ground, then I reached the "Engine Idle Check."

"Okay, don't read it to me yet," Beauregard told me, "We've got to be at altitude."

He made the bird rise straight up, which – along with hovering – is probably the most unusual sensation of helicopter flight, when compared to fixed-wing aircraft; it just feels *unnatural*. I watched the ground drop away through the Plexiglas bubble at my feet, my unease growing as the air temperature dropped noticeably.

"So we're going to go up to about 3,000 feet, then put the engine on 'idle,' and it tests the aircraft's ability to remain airborne without power."

I looked over at him, eyebrows raised.

"Or, well..." he struggled to think of a way to explain it to me. "Basically what it means is that we'll be falling, but not that fast. You'll hardly feel it."

Expert reassurances notwithstanding, this test sounded like one we should be doing *much* closer to the ground. Technically, I knew that helicopters were designed to remain airborne even if the engine fails: as long as the rotors are spinning, lift is being generated – if much more weakly – and the aircraft's descent is slowed to a certain degree. This knowledge, however, was not at all comforting as I watched the altimeter continue to roll upwards. We were nearing 3,000 feet now, and I could see the entire FOB spread out below me, with the mud-colored roofs of Ad Duluiyah to the south, and beyond it, the Tigris River with its green-shrouded banks, shining in the afternoon sunlight. It was a beautiful sight, but the fact that we were only moving up and not forward was still unsettling to me. As was the height itself.

Finally, Chief Beauregard had me read him the instructions, and he toggled the necessary controls to idle the engine, the roar of the engine changing pitch noticeably. He was right about the falling part – I could hardly tell we were losing altitude, although the altimeter told me we were dropping at about 10 feet per second. I was just starting to relax when a warning alarm started beeping insistently over the intercom system.

"What's that?" I asked.

Chief Beauregard punched a few buttons. "Looks like there's an issue with the engine sump."

I decided to let him focus on flying and not bother asking what the hell an engine 'sump' was. Chances were, I didn't want to know anyways. He kicked in the engine, slowing our descent, then turned to me. "Let's try that test again."

"Okay," I said, glancing back down at the flipbook on my knee. "Set engine to IDLE and note descent rate on altimeter," I read. "If descent rate exceeds…"

Beauregard had set it to idle again, and I felt the gentle drop as the altimeter began cycling through numbers. The warning beeps started again, immediately.

"There's that sump again," Chief Beauregard told me, flicking a switch to silence the warning alarm. He sat thinking for a moment, as I watched the altimeter continue to spin, the ground rising to meet us. "Is there a section in there called 'Warnings' or 'Cautions'?" He asked.

I flipped hurriedly forward – there was. I read aloud.

"If engine sump warning sounds, land immediately for crew safety."

"Huh," he said, managing to sound both indifferent and slightly disappointed. "Okay, looks like we failed that check, so we better set down."

We did so without issue, and I clambered awkwardly out of the seat as Chief Beauregard shut down the aircraft. I'd never been so glad to be standing on Iraqi sand. Dave came out of the bunker nearby and walked up, taking his flight helmet and vest as I handed them to him.

"How was it?" He asked.

"Awesome," I said, "until we failed the engine sump check and had to set down."

"Oh, no shit? Engine sump, interesting…I don't think I've seen that one before."

He wandered off to learn more from Chief Beauregard. I was happy to catch my breath for a moment and enjoy the sensation of still being alive.

*   *   *

Christmas in Iraq is about as depressing as it gets. Headquarters gave everyone the day off, except for the Kiowas, who selflessly flew non-stop patrols around the FOB to deter any attacks while the guard posts were empty, but that extra time to ourselves just gave us all that much more time to realize how far from home we were, and how much we missed our loved ones. It rained steadily throughout the day to punctuate the mood, turning the sand into clay-like mud in the Iraqi version of a "white" Christmas.

My fiancée and my family had sent me an immense amount of packages in preparation for the day, which we all appreciated – I shared about a dozen boxes of snacks and goodies with my platoon. Captain Hoffman had held a room-decorating contest, and some of the guys really got into it (first prize was an entire day off from operations), somehow getting hold of tinsel, fake Christmas trees, lights, the whole nine yards. Sergeant First Class Peterson completed his decorations by stealing a large inflatable fabric snowman from the top of a building on one of the big support FOBs. Someone else made a fake chimney out of a painted box, and arranged it to look like Santa was heading down it headfirst, his legs and combat boots kicking high in the air.

I opened my presents and ate lunch at the chow hall before calling home to thank everyone for my presents. The brief conversation made me more homesick, however. I was watching one of my new

131

DVDs in my room when I heard a knock on the door, and opened it to find my platoon, formed up in the rain, facing my door.

"Uhh…" I stammered. "What's up, guys?"

I was half-expecting a Christmas "rolling up" (the tradition of hazing Lieutenants), but under Staff Sergeant Barnes' direction, they broke into a rousing rendition of "Rudolph the Red-Nosed Reindeer," followed by another carol which nearly stalled midway through due to poorly-remembered lyrics. I had to grin – it was just what I needed. I had been Scrooging about, feeling lonely and sorry for myself, when all along I had been surrounded by the closest friends I would ever have. After they were done, I went to go thank Barnes and Neathery for the caroling.

"Don't sweat it, sir – those boys owed it to you, with all those packages you've been handing out," Barnes told me.

"I can't take credit for that," I replied, "That's all on my family back home."

"Well, I'm just saying…not every platoon has that."

The conversation shifted, and we talked about what we had purchased online to ship home for our loved ones for Christmas. Barnes wanted to send his wife something more than he already had, but he was out of ideas.

"What do you think, Dex? You're the one with the college degree – what should I get her?"

I scratched my head, deciding to have some fun. "…well, I dunno. You could go kinky."

Barnes snorted. "Yeah, that's good. Here ya go, honey, I decided to 'go kinky' this year, hope you like it! A big dildo with a bow on it. Good one, sir."

Neathery and I laughed.

Barnes moved on. "You know what pisses me off, though? You know what my mother-in-law always gets us for Christmas? Instead of just one nice present, every year, she goes and drops like 30 bucks at the dollar store, and we get a box full of cheap-ass junk."

*   *   *

Later that month, Staff Sergeant Barnes and I drew several weeks of Quick Reaction Force duty, which meant keeping our Bradleys parked near the Squadron headquarters at all times, ready to roll if we were needed for a special mission. On the second day, Squadron called us up. I jogged out to the road, where the Bradleys were starting up, and found Captain Hoffman with a satellite printout in his hand. He looked excited.

"Okay," he said, "Intelligence has a lead on one of the Turkey brothers."

I smiled, "Oh yeah, those guys!" The Turkey brothers were known insurgents that lived in the local town of Ad Duluiyah – I had led a raid of their home several weeks before, without success.

"This is a big deal: this mission is all the way from Washington," Hoffman continued, a little out of breath. "We're tracking his cell phone's location. I need you to conduct a hasty raid on his house to capture him."

"Okay sir, but I just have two Bradleys in my patrol. Are we getting any other support for this?"

"Negative – there's no one else available."

"I'm not going to be able to cordon off that target building at all," I warned him.

"Just do your best," he said. I could hear the aggravation in his voice.

"Roger, sir."

"Leave as soon as possible." He headed back to Squadron headquarters, and I called my soldiers in, giving them a quick lowdown on the mission.

"Cordon and search?" Barnes said, looking meaningfully around at the eight of us. "With who?"

I laughed. "That's what I said. It's just us."

"Okay, whatever. Do we at least know which house it is?"

"Yeah, it's the same one we hit last month, remember?"

Barnes frowned at me. "Sir, I didn't go to no college – I can't remember which damn house we hit!"

It was typical self-deprecating Barnes. Just a few days prior, while out on a routine patrol, he had noticed an Iraqi man hiding one arm in his shirt. Barnes had remembered that Squadron's Most Wanted list included a one-handed man, so they stopped and pulled his arm out of his shirt – the man was missing a hand. *Bad memory, my ass.*

"Okay, well I remember where the house is, so I'll lead the way," I told him, which was what he had wanted all along.

"Fine," he said. "I'll take your gunner and the dismounted scouts and clear the house when we reach the target, you guys can cover us from road with the Bradleys. Let's do this bullshit."

We loaded up and headed out the gate, pushing the Bradleys hard. It might have been a ridiculous mission, but we'd give it a shot. I took us straight to the house, stopping in front and blocking traffic on the main road. Wasser hopped out of the gunner's hatch next to me, joining the dismount team and Staff Sergeant Barnes on the ground. As they kicked in the door, I reported our status to headquarters. They came out a few minutes later, empty-handed, and after a cursory search of the area around the building, Wasser climbed back onto the turret, shaking his head.

"Nothing, sir."

"Roger." I reported in, and we headed back to FOB Mackenzie. Twenty minutes later, we pulled in through the front gate, and I was about to hop down to clear my weapons, when Bulldawg X-Ray came on the troop net.

"Red 1, X-Ray – hold at your current location."

"Here we go again," Barnes told me on our platoon net.

Hoffman hurried over to us, even more excited this time, and I met him behind my Bradley.

"We got another update from Washington – the NSA is monitoring his cell phone conversations. He was talking to some guy on the phone when you got there, and he told the guy that he had to leave his house because soldiers were coming for him! You guys almost got him!"

I was tempted to remind him of the famous Army phrase that "almost" only counts in horseshoes and hand grenades, but before I could say anything, Hoffman spoke again.

"I want you to go back and hit the house again, but this time I want you to search some of the surrounding area, too – chances are he's still right in that area and hasn't gone far."

"Sir, I agree, but I can't cordon off a whole city block with four scouts and two vehicles with skeleton crews," I told him. "Are there any helicopters up…or anyone else that can augment us?"

"Negative," he said, frowning.

"We don't have a picture of this guy," I went on. "So now that he's left his house, we could drive right past him and not even know it. The only identifying feature we have is the fact that he has a cell phone, and all he has to do is toss it…"

Impatient, Hoffman cut me off. "Lieutenant Platt, don't be so negative."

I realized that I could argue all afternoon with no effect, so I climbed back into my turret and we headed out again. As we drove back into town, Barnes and I put together a plan over the radio that would somewhat accomplish the intent of the mission. He stopped a block short of the target, while I pushed on a block past the house. Covering them with the Bradleys, we then kicked out our dismounted scouts, who patrolled slowly up the street, the two halves of the patrol converging on the target building. It was a pretty meager net – though they checked down alleys and side streets, and searched military age males as they encountered them, we all felt frustrated at the futility of it all. It was clearly an important mission – this guy was a known insurgent with a rap sheet long enough to have put him on Washington's radar, and yet all we could muster to try to catch him was eight soldiers in two Bradleys, because everyone else was too busy out securing routes and escorting supply convoys. If there was ever an argument for needing more troops in Iraq, this was it.

We didn't find the Turkey brother, of course, but there was a silver lining to this cloud. Because of all the unwanted attention he was getting from us in Ad Duluiyah, Mr. Turkey left town that day, fleeing across the Tigris into 1-77 Armor's area of operations. They pinpointed his cell phone location again at a farmhouse out in the countryside, and 1-77 was able to raid the place. This time, since the target house was isolated and 1-77 scraped together enough forces to do it properly, he did not escape.

*   *   *

After Christmas, Squadron decided to piggyback on the success of Operation Baton Rouge in Samarra, and launch a massive series of raids in the local towns outside FOB Mackenzie. Bulldawg Troop was assigned several targets in Ad Montessim, the same town where my first raid leading Red Platoon had taken place, not far from the checkpoint we had manned during Operation Baton Rouge.

With three platoons still tied up manning the checkpoints outside Samarra, that left my platoon plus First Lieutenant Thomas' and Sergeant First Class Peterson's mortars to conduct the raid on our own – and it was a complex one. We would attempt three coordinated, simultaneous raids on opposite sides of the town: while the Mortars platoon hit a house in the town itself, my platoon would take down two buildings on the outskirts, one targeting an artillery Colonel from the former Iraqi Army who was suspected of masterminding rocket attacks on FOB Mackenzie, and the other looking for a man who acted as a driver for one of the insurgent leaders in Samarra.

We approached the town from opposite directions, but managed to hit our targets just as the Mortars hit theirs. Staff Sergeant Barnes led the ground team going after the Colonel, while just down the block, Sergeant Landry's team kicked in the chauffeur's door. The Colonel was not at home, and while they started a thorough search of his house, Sergeant Landry's team reported "dry hole" (no one home) as well. Landry, however, soon found contraband: wires, detonators, and AK-47s, and as they were gathering this up, an Eagle Troop air weapons team raised me on the troop net.

"Bulldawg Red 1, Eagle 33: we have a squirter identified in the weeds west of the target house, over."

I relayed the message to Landry on the ground, who pushed his team outside and quickly tracked the man down, aided by the infrared spotlight from the helicopter. As they were bringing him in, we got another report of a "squirter" from Squadron headquarters – apparently we had a fighter jet on station, and his imaging system had picked up a guy fleeing from a house we hadn't even sent a team to. The pilot sent us the grid coordinates via Squadron, but by the time I was able to move Staff Sergeant Barnes' team there, the guy had displaced. I could see us playing this game all night – asking where he was, waiting several minutes for the location to get relayed to us, having him move before we got there – and apparently, so could the fighter pilot, because he activated a laser designator as my scouts were regrouping. It was invisible to the naked eye, but through night vision goggles it looked like an alien death ray, a massive beam of green light streaking out of the empty sky, winking on and off repeatedly and designating the man's location.

Barnes' team worked their way through the weeds again, following the beam, but to their chagrin they found the man had swum across a canal. They backtracked to a bridge, slogged back to the crossing site, and followed the trail of wet grass up to a house nearby. In the front yard was a pile of wet clothes. On the doorstep, a pair of waterlogged, muddy sandals. And inside, when they cleared the house, there was a slightly damp man in bed, pretending to sleep.

"Nice try, dick," Barnes told him, before handcuffing him and marching him outside.

*   *   *

With our tour in Iraq almost up, 1st Infantry Division was already thinking ahead to how it would move 10,000 soldiers and all their vehicles and equipment back to Germany. At the troop level, this transportation planning is conducted by a platoon leader who's assigned to be the Unit Movement Officer as an extra duty. Unfortunately for me, Lieutenant Taylor had been the UMO when we deployed, and Captain Hoffman had picked me to replace him. First, however, I would need to be trained and certified by attending a week-long course in Kuwait.

It's hard to complain about an assignment that gets you out of combat and caught up on sleep with three hot meals a day, but I was reluctant to leave my men. I trusted my NCOs fully to run things in my absence, but as a leader, it ran against my instincts to disappear for a week to Kuwait in the midst of an arduous operation. I registered my complaints, but they were overruled, and the next day I found myself on a Blackhawk heading for FOB Speicher, where I would be catching a C-130 on to Kuwait, along with Staff Sergeant Lapierre from Blue Platoon, who would be taking a course on Hazardous Materials handling procedures to assist me.

Flying in Iraq is closer to hitch-hiking than anything else. You arrive at the airfield, put your name on a list to be added to the next flight going in your direction, and wait until they call your name. There's never a set schedule, and your flight is rarely going directly to your destination. This happened to be the case for my flight to Kuwait, which was routed through Baghdad first.

We made a combat landing in Baghdad at about 9 p.m. that evening, the pilot dropping us into a brutally sharp descent before leveling out at the last minute and touching down on the tarmac at Baghdad International Airport. In Baghdad, to my surprise, we took on about 40 Iraqi policemen, who looked like little kids on Christmas morning as they climbed excitedly aboard – for most, it was their first-ever flight. I wandered over to one of the Air Force crewmen, who was double-checking the locking mechanism keeping our baggage pallet in place on the aft ramp.

"Hey, Sergeant," I asked, "What's the deal with the cops?"

He shrugged, "I think they've been selected for some special training."

"In Kuwait?" I asked, incredulous. I couldn't see any way the Kuwaitis were going to pay for or run police training for Iraqis – they all still remembered 1991 fairly vividly.

"No, in Jordan," he told me. "We're routing through Jordan first. Didn't you guys know?"

My Middle East geography wasn't great, but I realized that our flight plan would be like flying through Chicago to get from New York to Miami. Resigned to a long night of flying, I headed back to my seat. The Iraqis fared well on their first flight – a couple started to look a little green, especially as we juked through more evasive maneuvers on takeoff, but no one blew chunks. This would not have been the case had they stayed on for the final leg into Kuwait. There were only about 15 of us left on the flight when we took off from Jordan, so we were able to stretch out along the canvas benches and try to sleep. About halfway to Kuwait, however, we ran into a freak thunderstorm over the desert.

I've been on planes in bad turbulence and storms before, but this was on a completely different level. Whether due to the nature of the storm, or the flight performance of a C-130 versus a civilian jet, I don't know. Either way, we spent a solid hour rocking and rolling through what felt and sounded like a hurricane. I was asleep when we hit the first patch of turbulence, and I literally came out of my seat, weightless for an instant as the plane went into free-fall. I slammed down *hard* when we bottomed out, and learned my lesson well – I spent the rest of the time sitting upright, and later buckled my seat belt, too. It felt like an unending, completely unpredictable roller coaster ride, but though I felt queasy immediately, I managed to avoid puking. I talked to one of the crew chiefs after half an hour of stomach-churning drops.

"This is pretty bad, right?" I had to shout to be heard over the engine noise.

He considered for a second, then nodded. "Yeah. It's not the worst I've seen, but it's definitely in the top ten."

"Great!" I told him, sarcastically.

"The Lieutenant's flying, otherwise it might be a little smoother," he said, meaning that the more experienced pilot had decided to let his junior officer fly in order to gain experience. That didn't help allay my fears at all. We suddenly hit a particularly deep hole, and I felt the plane drop fast again, the sickening free-fall lasting for several seconds. I shook my head, wide-eyed.

"Jesus!"

The airman grinned, "That was a good one, sir! Probably a couple hundred foot drop!"

We made it to Kuwait a little bruised and battered, and thankfully I had a week in which to try to repress those memories, before I would have to fly back to Iraq.

CHAPTER TEN

"They gave me the malaria pills, and I was standing there, looking
at the bottle, when I had this 'Eureka!' moment. I threw those
bitches right out! I've got a shitload of mosquito bites...I figure if it
all works out, I'll get out of this shithole for at least 4 months.
Malaria's like mono: it comes back now and then,
but that ain't so bad, really."
-Lieutenant Joey Thomas

In Kuwait, I learned what I could about transportation logistics –
mostly, what paperwork I needed to fill out to ensure that our tanks
didn't get shipped to Hawaii by accident – caught up on sleep, and
when the class was finished, made the return journey to FOB
Mackenzie. The morning after I got back, I led my platoon north to
FOB Wilson, where we were to be attached to Charlie "Rock"
Troop.

Rock Troop was commanded by Captain Young and his
Executive Officer, Dan Cho, who were a blast to work for – smart
and sensible, they were both natural leaders with a keen sense of
humor. In fact, Rock Troop had already had a great deal of
amusement at our commander's expense. Captain Young's fiancée
and Captain Hoffman's wife had gone on vacation together to the
Mediterranean earlier in the year, which gave Young an excellent idea.
He sent Hoffman an email after the women returned, commenting
on how hot the topless photos of the two women had been.
Hoffman, not realizing his chain was being yanked, flipped out and

left his wife a bitter voicemail message and a scathing email to boot.

Hoffman wasn't the only target of their pranks – Charlie Troop also stole a Notre Dame flag from one of the Squadron staff officers, who was an alumnus and outspoken football fan. For the rest of the rotation, they emailed him photos of his Notre Dame flag turning up in the wackiest places: flying atop the Iraqi Police station, next to an AK-47 found under a mattress during a raid, held up by three grinning detainees after another raid. The staff officer took it well, which may be why they preferred to target Hoffman – he reacted. The two of them endlessly urged me to tease Hoffman for them when I returned to FOB Mackenzie.

"You gotta ask him when they're going to take the training wheels off," Cho told me, referring to Hoffman's junior status among the rest of the commanders.

I laughed. "Yeah, I'll get right on that, Dan."

Young chimed in: "No, this is what you have to do – in the middle of a troop meeting, when he briefs a plan for something, just shake your head and go, 'hmmm.' Then when he's like, 'What?' You can say, 'No, it's nothing, sir…it's just…I don't think Captain Young would do it that way.'" Which was probably true.

Dan Cho's penchant for insubordination wasn't limited to pranks on officers in the Squadron. Units in combat are always assigned clearly delineated areas of operation, to ensure that just one commander "owns" that terrain. Just as airline pilots check in with various air traffic controllers as they move along their route, units out on operations are required to check in with the command center that controls an area of operations if they move into that sector. This ensures that everyone knows when there are friendlies in the area, and reduces the likelihood of a friendly fire incident. Charlie Troop's area of operations was the collection of small towns where Saddam was eventually captured, directly across the river from Tikrit, where 1-18 Infantry operated.

For some reason, 1-18 Infantry formed a habit of driving over the bridge across the Tigris and surreptitiously patrolling or conducting a raid in Charlie Troop's sector. A Charlie Troop patrol would be out checking the roads for IEDs, and suddenly see a bunch of Humvees disgorging infantrymen into a building in their town. As Troop Executive Officer, it was Dan Cho's responsibility to run the Charlie Troop operations center, and after the first few times this happened, he politely called 1-18 and reminded them that it was not only common courtesy but in the best interests of their soldier's long-term health that they notify him when they were in his area of operations. When it happened again, he lost his shit.

Dan called up 1-18 on the field phone and asked to speak with their Operations Officer, who was not only fifteen years his senior, but also outranked him by two full pay grades.

"This is Major Collins."

"Sir, this is Lieutenant Cho over in Charlie Troop, 1-4 CAV. I was just notified by one of my patrols that there is a 1-18 unit in my area of operations…again. That makes the third time this month, sir, that your units have entered my battle space without checking in with my operations center. I could understand it if the boundary between us was just an arbitrary line on the map – mistakes happen, sir. But it's the FUCKING TIGRIS RIVER! Please ensure your units maintain standard reporting procedures from now on."

With that, he slammed the phone down, checked his watch, then sat down to wait. It took all of three minutes for the phone to ring again. He got an ass-chewing from our Squadron chain of command, but they knew he was in the right, and 1-18 Infantry never crossed the Tigris again.

*　　　*　　　*

We were attached to Charlie Troop to assist them in the upcoming elections, Iraq's first free and democratic vote since the fall of Saddam. From the start of our tour, 1st Infantry Division headquarters had been hyping the crucial importance of these elections, with good reason. For a country mired in what was looking more and more like civil war, where our presence was becoming less tolerated and more resented by the day, a successful democratic election had the potential to reverse the downward spiral and set the country on the right path towards security and self-sufficiency.

For better or worse, our commanders had linked the success of our deployment with the success of the elections, so we all viewed them as our final exam of the tour, our last chance to salvage something from the months of frustration and stalled progress, something we might all believe was worth the sacrifices that had been made. It was a gamble, and we knew it: if all the citizens were too scared, too intimidated, or too indifferent to come out and vote, it would feel like a wasted year.

After we settled into our quarters at FOB Wilson, Sergeant First Class Martin and I attended a Charlie Troop meeting to discuss the upcoming operation. It would not be easy – while Anvil's sector in the south included nine polling sites which were relatively tightly clustered in and around Ad Duluiyah, Rock Troop's area of operations included no less than 16 polling sites, some as far as three hours' drive away by Humvee. Securing them all was impossible, even with Iraqi assistance, so Rock's commander, Captain Young, had determined the ones that would be most prone to insurgent attack, and divided them equally among his forces. All 16 sites would have to be visited both before and after the elections, however, in order to drop off the ballots and voting equipment, and then later to pick up the completed ballots and deliver them to the processing center in Tikrit.

As an additional wrinkle, while we were ultimately responsible for the security of the polling sites, the Iraqi Army and Police would be the only forces present at each site. This was an Iraqi event, so it would be kept safe by Iraqis, and no one wanted it to look like the Americans were forcing people to vote or tampering in any way with the electoral process. We would help enforce the curfew the night before, and we could help them plan and set up security, but little more. During the actual elections, we would take up positions in hide sites nearby, close enough to the polling sites to lend immediate assistance if necessary, but otherwise invisible to the general populace, except for a few short trips to each site to ensure everything was running smoothly.

I split my platoon into two sections – Martin and Barnes would lead the three Bradleys in one section, and I would take our three up-armored Humvees in the other, Staff Sergeant Landry serving as my wingman. The following morning, with Major Randall from Squadron staff leading the patrol, we escorted several cargo trucks to the farthest polling sites out by the Jabal Hamrin ridge, where we had conducted our troop area reconnaissance so many months before. It was a long, hot drive, and we stopped along the way at three or four rural schools to meet with the local sheikh, imam, or mayor – whoever was in charge – to hand off the voting equipment and check

143

security arrangements. Each site received several thousand ballots and flyers describing (in Arabic) the voting process and the candidates running for election, as well as several large plastic tubs to hold the ballots, cardboard dividers to serve as privacy booths, and some posters to put up around town. Major Randall engaged the local leaders in conversation with the help of an interpreter, while my team and I pulled security, unloaded the equipment, and gave each site a quick once-over, looking for anything that might indicate an attack was planned.

On the eve of the elections, we moved out to our hide site near the town of Al Alam, stopping by the nearest site to let the Iraqi Police Captain know that we were there if he needed us. It was a long, mainly sleepless night, all of us dozing in our Humvee seats, weapons at the ready. Dawn was bitterly cold. We stamped our feet on the frozen mud, blowing on our hands to warm up. I heated up my breakfast MRE, and when it was warm, stuck the heating pack inside my uniform as a hot water bottle. By the afternoon it would warm up to about 60 degrees, forcing us to peel off layers throughout the day, but winter nights in the desert were hovering around freezing. Voting wasn't scheduled to start for another couple hours, so we took the chance to shave – using the side-mirrors on the Humvee for help – brush our teeth, and relieve ourselves in preparation for the long day ahead.

I was impatient to see what the turnout would be for the vote, but I waited until just before voting was scheduled to begin to take the Humvees down to the polling site, wanting to minimize our presence at the beginning of the day. We walked into complete chaos in the schoolhouse – about the only good news was that most of the town seemed to be there, and seemed to be enthusiastic about being there, but the organizers were still at least 30 minutes away from having everything set up. The election officials who had been trained how to put everything together had waited until the last minute to arrive, and the impatient townspeople had started putting the whole operation together themselves. It shouldn't have been a surprise, really – the concept of punctuality is somewhat foreign to Iraqis, especially compared to the U.S. military.

In every room, three or four men were loudly talking and ripping open boxes full of supplies, their heavy winter coats looking comically incongruous over their night-shirt-like dishdashas and sandals. I poked around for a few minutes, then found the police chief, who was arguing with an older man in a red-and-white-checked head-scarf. The police chief excused himself when he saw me, looked around at the chaos, shrugged, and smiled, as if to say, "What a mess, right?"

I hid my impatience and smiled back, nodding, but then he beckoned me to follow him to the back of the school, where he showed me an empty room with glass shards all over the floor. Through charades he made me understand that there had been an attack during the night. Several men had approached the school's outer wall, thrown grenades over the side of it, and run off under fire from the police guarding the school. No one had been hurt, the grenades had simply blown in the windows on this side of the building. The attack had clearly done little to blunt the local people's desire to vote, thankfully.

I sent the report up, and Captain Young, who was out in sector moving between his disparate units to check on progress, trekked up north to see the damage for himself. While we were walking around the outside of the building, Captain Young spotted a grenade body that hadn't exploded, and we called EOD in to deal with it, clearing everyone out of that side of the building for safety. A half hour later, EOD rolled in, and their NCO sauntered around the school to the unexploded grenade. He bent over it for a second, peering closely at it, then picked it up and put it in his cargo pocket.

"Okay, we'll see you guys later," he said.

Young and I shared a look – *crazy-ass EOD!*

Though the leader and organizer in me was dying to establish order and get voting started quickly, we mounted up and left the Iraqis to figure the voting out on their own, heading south to the second polling site, which was running a bit more smoothly. Our morning checks completed, we returned to the hide site to rest and kill some more time. All other polling sites were reporting steady activity, which hinted at success, but like a pitcher throwing a no-hitter, we were reluctant to discuss it and thereby jinx ourselves.

Instead, we talked about going home, the topic at the forefront of everyone's mind now that we were just five weeks away from our scheduled return. Though we knew it was a completely pointless exercise, we bandied about theories on exactly when we would be leaving, speculating and sharing rumors we had overheard. Just the thought that we were so close to going home was enough to put a smile on my face.

In the mid-afternoon, we did another round of checks, and this time found all as it should be at the sites: people were lining up in an orderly fashion (sometimes a hundred or more at a time), voting in the semi-privacy of the cardboard booths, and placing their ballots in the sealed containers after getting their fingers marked with ink. The mood in town was festive, and it wasn't just because no one was going to work that day – people were genuinely excited. For the first time during our tour, I saw adults waving and smiling at us. Granted, this small town was known for being a quiet sector, a well-to-do suburb of Tikrit whose citizens were mostly white-collar types with steady jobs and little incentive to take up arms. But we were willing to take any small victories we could get.

Across Iraq, things were not always as quiet, as the insurgents tried to undermine the election process with coordinated attacks on the Iraqis who turned out to vote. In Balad, a line of several hundred people formed at one of the busiest polling sites, and quickly came under insurgent mortar fire, the deadly rounds killing or injuring several civilians. While the Army responded, the dead and wounded were cared for, and the line of people, undeterred, stoically reassembled. One of my most potent memories of the day was seeing an ancient Iraqi woman emerge from the southern polling site, a triumphant, toothless grin on her weathered face, her ink-stained finger held high.

Finally, after sundown, the polls were closed, and we linked up with the cargo trucks once again to begin collecting the sealed ballot boxes for transport back to Tikrit, where they would be counted. At the northern site, despite their disorganization of the morning, the population had finished voting sooner, and they were ready for us, the Iraqi Police lending a hand as we tossed the boxes up onto the high cargo beds. I shook the police chief's hand, and he gripped mine firmly in return, touching his left hand to his heart in the traditional gesture of appreciation and respect.

Full dark had fallen by the time we left for the southern polling site, where a power outage in town forced them to break out flashlights and oil lamps to help see what they were doing. Here the air was downright celebratory – I tried to make my way inside to try to find someone in charge and start collecting the ballot boxes, but I was stopped numerous times by Iraqi soldiers and civilians, laughing and clapping me on the back.

"America good! Go U.S.A.!" They shouted.

After months of indifference or hostility, it was an amazing change, and felt indescribably satisfying to see them appreciate something we had helped them achieve. I smiled back, shaking hands all around.

"Iraq good!" I told them, trying to make it clear that it was their success, not ours – they had braved the threat of attacks to come out and vote.

I was still laughing and smiling when I walked into the large room where most of the work seemed to be focused. At first I was confused at what was going on – the ballot boxes were open, men were frantically counting papers and bundling them with rubber bands into rolls of 100 ballots, and my first assumption was that those were leftover ballots. I wandered up to the nearest man, and saw the ballots he was counting were all filled out.

"Oh, shit! Stop! Stopstopstop!!"

They halted and looked at me, annoyed that I was interrupting them – couldn't I see that they were busy? I motioned to them to put the ballots back in the boxes, to seal them up again and stop counting. They were confused, shaking their heads and speaking rapidly.

"English? Anyone speak English?"

There was an Iraqi soldier who had a smattering of English, so we roped him inside and, haltingly, I had him translate for me.

"You must put away the ballots. They are secret – you understand, secret? No one can look at them."

It took a few tries and some charades, but he got the idea, and told the men in the room. They argued back, vehemently.

"Uh, they say…Tikrit tell them…" he gestured on his fingers, miming like he was counting them, "…all papers."

I shook my head, "No!" I picked up the nearest ballot box, showing the seal that they had broken in the act of opening it. "Once someone votes, no one else sees it until Tikrit."

Eventually, I convinced them to stop – they weren't trying to rig the election or get an early count or anything nearly as sophisticated as that, but somehow they had gotten the message to count ballots. The ballot boxes were translucent, so it's possible that the instructions had been to get a rough estimate by looking into the boxes, or to count voters, but I never knew for sure. The seals were broken on a number of boxes, whose ballots were clearly tampered with, lying as they did in neatly counted rolls, but there was nothing more I could do about it – presumably, the officials in Tikrit would either throw out the votes (I hoped not) or write it all off as a rookie error and count them anyway. We loaded up the boxes, visited one last site to load up, and then escorted the trucks back to FOB Wilson.

On base, though we were all tired, there was an air of accomplishment as well, everyone quietly satisfied in the knowledge that we'd been a part of history, had helped to secure a nation's first free elections, and were about to go home. Captain Young and Major Randall found me soon after we returned, having heard my radio report about the ballot counting. I gave them a full account of what had happened, adding my opinion that it was an act of ignorance and misunderstanding, not willful wrongdoing. They agreed, but could not guarantee what would happen to the ballets in Tikrit – it was an Iraqi civil matter, after all. In all, nearly 6,000 Iraqis turned out to vote at our two polling sites that day. Across the country, the citizens turned out in droves, traveling many miles and often at great risk to make their voice be heard.

My other section had been busy, too. The hide site Sergeant First Class Martin picked for his Bradleys was not far from an isolated house on the eastern side of the town of Ad Dawr. Late that night, Sergeant Newsome noticed a car moving towards the house, its headlights off. That was not entirely unusual – many cars had broken headlights in Iraq – but it could also indicate he was trying to avoid attention. Rather than intercept it straight away, Martin decided to maintain the element of surprise, merely tracking its progress through their long-range thermal sights. Once at the house, the driver parked, opened his trunk, and began digging in his backyard. As soon as they positively identified that he was in fact unearthing a weapons cache, they thundered in and surrounded the building and car, searching both and detaining the man. It was a significant cache – mortar and RPG rounds, rifles, grenade launchers – the usual Soviet arsenal. In the car, they also found a digital video camera, which contained several hours of footage of Rock Troop patrols in and around the city, surreptitiously recorded as preliminary intelligence-gathering prior to an attack. As they later discovered, their captive was a high value target who had been on the wanted list for some months. It was the perfect cap to a successful operation.

CHAPTER ELEVEN

"Okay: White 4, this is Bulldawg X-Ray...you're coming in
broken. All I made out was something about 'All they need to know
is' and then a bunch of static, and then 'so tell them to pull their
heads out of their asses.' Say again, over."
-Bulldawg Troop command post NCO

Sadly, we left Rock Troop immediately after the elections and
returned to FOB Mackenzie. As we rolled in the main gate, we
found our path blocked by a line of vehicles waiting to enter. It took
us a minute, but we suddenly realized they were from 3rd Infantry
Division – *our replacements were here!* Task Force 1-15 Infantry would
be replacing us at Mackenzie, and their advance party had just
arrived. Our mission was now to secure their movement as their
main body began arriving from Kuwait, and start training them up to
replace us, just as 4th Infantry Division had done for us at the
beginning of our rotation. The relief-in-place operation was
scheduled to last several weeks, at the end of which time we would
begin our own movement out of theater.

In preparation for receiving Task Force 1-15, we moved out of
our rooms and into a tent village built as a temporary housing area.
We grumbled a bit about losing our nice accommodations, but it's
hard to be sour at guys who also represent your ticket home. We
continued to grumble about Captain Hoffman's leadership of the
troop, however – it seemed that the closer we got to going home, the
more stubborn he became, seemingly inventing new ways to bother

us with time-wasting tasks and useless rules. It got to the point that my fellow scout platoon leader, Ryan Simms, and I would look at each other during meetings, trying not to laugh as we listened to the latest bullshit. The outspoken Sergeant First Class Nicholls was not so well-behaved, and like all of us, took particular umbrage at the fact that our troop seemed to inherit more than its fair share of extra assignments from Squadron Headquarters. It seemed like every time he went to Squadron for a meeting, Captain Hoffman came back with another extra duty or mission for us – he was incapable of telling his superiors that we were over-worked and undermanned, and we ended up suffering for it.

Finally, after a particularly loud argument, Captain Hoffman said: "Sergeant Nicholls: if you don't have anything constructive to say, and you're just going to complain, you can just leave."

Nicholls had had enough. "Okay," he said, and walked out.

I had my own showdown with Hoffman soon after. Half of my platoon was running daily trips to the nearest logistics base and back in our Humvees, serving as guides and convoy escorts for the 1-15 Infantry convoys coming into sector. At the same time, I was running route clearance missions along the road to Samarra in the south, and maintaining observation posts at night in the same area to search for insurgents laying IEDs. When we weren't out on mission, I was running around FOB Mackenzie arranging for the movement of all of the troop's equipment back to Germany, while my soldiers tried to squeeze in much-needed maintenance on our burned-out vehicles, and start packing up their own gear and equipment. We were tapped out.

Task Force 1-15's supply NCO arrived on one of the first convoys, since he had to inventory and sign for the equipment that we would be leaving behind for them to use. That included our up-armor Humvees, but before we signed them over, Captain Hoffman made an announcement.

"I want them to be inspection-ready. I want everyone to go to the wash rack and clean out their Humvees, just as if we were in garrison."

We were incredulous. We had planned to clean them before we handed them over for the final time (that's just good manners), but not for the inventory: we still needed to use those Humvees for the next few weeks until we left. We couldn't figure out why Hoffman wanted to impress some Staff Sergeant from the incoming company, who didn't honestly care what the trucks looked like, as long as the serial numbers matched his paperwork. My soldiers were already operating on about four hours of sleep a night, and now they would have to lose more sleep, spend several hours washing our vehicles, and then soon afterwards take those same vehicles back out on mission, where they would be filthy dirty again in a matter of minutes…and then a couple of weeks later, we would have to wash them again! When Captain Hoffman quickly silenced my objections in the meeting, I decided not to argue the point any further, knowing it would get me absolutely nowhere. Sergeant First Class Martin and I walked back to the tents together.

"This is a new low for Captain Hoffman, sir."

"I know it," I replied, fuming. "Fuck that, I'm not wasting my soldiers' time like that. My job is to protect them from bullshit, right?"

Martin was quiet, letting me vent.

"We're not going to do it," I told him firmly.

He shrugged. "The boys will get it done if you tell them to, sir."

"I know they will," I said, my anger softening a little. I made up my mind and called them all together for the evening brief. At the end, I took a deep breath.

"Okay, last on the agenda, the commander wants us to take the up-armor Humvees to the washrack before the inspection the day after tomorrow." There was a low murmur, and I saw a couple of my soldiers shaking their heads in disgust. Staff Sergeant Barnes raised his hand. I waved him away, knowing he was going to raise the same points I had already made to the commander.

"…but we're not going to do that," I continued. Martin raised his eyebrows at me, but stayed quiet. "If the commander asks you guys why you didn't wash the trucks, you can just tell him I told you not to. Questions?"

There were none. Most of them were too tired to find much humor in the situation – after a full year of such bullshit, they just wanted to finish the job and go home. I let them go, but Barnes beckoned me over as they dispersed.

"Why are you picking a fight with the commander, sir?"

"I already tried to talk sense into the Lieutenant, Barnes, he doesn't want to listen," Martin interjected.

I answered Barnes: "Because I'm tired of his crap."

"Took you this long?" Barnes asked, grinning.

I laughed. "No. It's just taken this long for me to be able to do something concrete about it."

He was serious for a second. "He ain't gonna like this, sir."

"Whatever," I said, "I don't care if he slams me for it, I'm getting out of the Army, anyways."

Barnes shook his head and gave me a look that said: *it's your funeral.*

In retrospect, we should have played it differently – we could have blamed the dirty Humvees on poor internal communications in the platoon, or any number of vague but generally more excusable reasons. I tried to make myself scarce when the inspection rolled around, but about 15 minutes after it started one of the operations center crew found me in our tent, doing paperwork. Apparently, the commander wanted to see me.

"I wonder why?" I asked sarcastically, picking up my rifle and flak vest. He grinned back at me – word had got out.

Captain Hoffman was inspecting the mechanics' Humvee when I walked up, loudly praising them for the cleanliness of their vehicle and the obvious care they had taken to make it so.

"You wanted to see me, sir?" I asked, innocently.

"Lieutenant Platt, I need to talk to you." Hoffman pulled me off to the side, but not far enough that we were out of earshot of the soldiers nearby. *First mistake,* I thought to myself.

"Did I not tell you to clean and wash your Humvees at the last two troop meetings?" He asked.

"Yes, sir."

"Then why is it that your soldiers tell me you ordered them *not* to clean them yesterday?"

"Because I disagreed with your order, sir. It didn't make sense to me."

Straight-up insubordination, freely admitted. Hoffman was momentarily at a loss.

"Lieutenant Platt, I gave you a direct order, and we are in *combat...*" Hoffman had the good sense not to open up a debate on the merits of his order, at least, but he still hadn't raised his voice, and apart from blushing heavily, he wasn't really intimidating me at all. This was the nicest ass-chewing I'd ever had.

"…if you 'disagreed' with my order, you should have raised your objections to me, not just countermanded my order," he finished.

I was thinking: *I tried, and you just told me to shut the fuck up,* when I realized that he had just made his second mistake, and handed me my escape route on a silver platter.

"You're absolutely right, sir: I should have raised my objections. Next time I will, sir."

He could have pressed the issue, or fired me on the spot – technically he could have court-martialed me, though it would have been the most ridiculous court-martial in history. Instead, he backed down, as I had gambled he would: any disciplinary action he brought against me would have been made public to the entire Squadron, and Hoffman didn't want the world to know that he couldn't control his platoon leaders.

No more than a minute later, one of the operations center soldiers came outside to relay a message from Squadron headquarters: my Humvees were ordered to leave immediately to escort another Task Force 1-15 convoy, who was ready to move to FOB Mackenzie ahead of schedule. The NCO signing for my Humvees hadn't even had a chance to look at them yet, and would have to sign for them some other time – my scouts were already loading up and flipping their radios on. I barely suppressed my smile as I jumped in the nearest vehicle to join them.

*   *   *

Bulldawg Troop would be swapping out with C ("Crusader") Company from Task Force 1-15, under Captain Quinn, which included two Humvee-mounted infantry platoons and a platoon of tanks. Since they only had three platoons versus Bulldawg Troop's four, and my platoon was mainly running ad hoc missions, I wasn't assigned a platoon to train, which left me more time to finalize the troop's movement plans. Even those platoons that did have replacements to train struggled to find things to do to occupy their time – Blue, White and Green platoons were all responsible for the checkpoints outside Samarra at this point, which largely meant watching the Iraqi Army soldiers who were manning the checkpoints to make sure they were doing everything to standard, and otherwise simply remaining on site as a physical deterrent to attacks. My fellow scout platoon leader, Ryan Simms, summed it up perfectly:

"What exactly am I supposed to do with these guys from 1-15 when they 'mirror checkpoint operations?'" He asked me, rhetorically. "'Okay, here's what we do, guys: we sit here and fuck off, and every once in a while we walk over and yell at the Iraqi Army guys if they're not doing their job.'"

I ended up teaching the Crusader Company leadership a few classes on some new equipment we had been issued and "lessons learned" from raids and cordon & search operations. They were attentive and polite, and I couldn't help feeling sorry for them: not only because they were just beginning their rotation, but also because their three platoons were inheriting the same missions that we had barely been handling with four platoons.

Following my raid class, Hoffman tasked me to conduct an actual raid so that they could watch how we operated in the field, so I went to ask the Squadron Intelligence officer if he could find us a target. He was kind of confused – normally, when he received information about a target, he passed it on immediately and we took action on it right away.

He scratched his head, thinking. "Well, it's not like I have a list of bad guys sitting around that we've never tried to catch," he told me.

"I know," I said. "Look, honestly, sir? You can point to a random house on the map for all I care. We're just showing the 1-15 guys the ropes."

He nodded, "Okay, still…might as well send you to a valid target."

He sifted through some maps, then pulled out a printout that caught his eye. "Ah, this'll work – been there a couple times but he's never home, we think he probably skipped town permanently. Has ties to a cell leader in Samarra."

I looked at the map, studying the terrain. "Ad Montessim, huh? We know that area well. Good target building, too – isolated, outside of town, near the road. Thanks, sir."

He made me some color copies, gave me the target's name, and I headed back to the tent to relax for a while. Captain Hoffman wanted me to brief my plan to him and the Crusader Company officers that evening, but I'd done so many raids that I could make it up on the fly. There was likewise no need to give my soldiers anything other than a simple Warning Order – when we were leaving, who was going, what and where the mission was.

At around 6:30 the following morning, we lined up on the access road, two Bradleys with dismounts to clear the building. When Captain Hoffman and the Crusader leadership joined us, I gave a patrol brief for their benefit, and we headed out the gate, my Bradleys in the lead. It might have been a bullshit mission, but it was a beautiful day. The morning was cool, the wind brisk as I stood in my hatch, the turret swiveling purposefully below me as Wasser scanned danger areas with practiced ease. Suddenly, and with something of a shock, I realized I was going to miss all of this – the feeling of leaving on patrol, the adrenaline rush of leading a team of expert, veteran soldiers into unknown challenges ahead. I hadn't just become used to leading my platoon, I'd become *good at it,* and I found myself laughing out loud. *How the hell had I come to like it here?!*

We roared through Ad Montessim and slid through the turn onto the side road which held our target house. I gave my dismounts a 30-second warning over the intercom, checking my GPS against the map printouts as we neared the house. It emerged around the final turn, and I guided my Bradley past it before directing Schufeld to halt and drop the ramp. Behind me, Landry's Bradley was doing the same, and as I reported setting the inner cordon to Captain Hoffman, I saw Staff Sergeant Barnes lead one dismount team towards the house in a hunched-over sprint, rifles to their cheeks as they covered the windows and doors ahead of them. The other dismount team headed to the back of the house. As directed, Landry took his Bradley off-road to the far side of the house, not only to cover the dismounts' movement, but also to ensure that no one escaped from the house. I watched as Barnes' team kicked in the front door and flowed smoothly inside.

"Bulldawg 6, Red 1, my Eagles have entered the target building, over."

"This is 6, roger."

I checked my watch: Barnes had bet me they could clear the house in under 30 seconds. At the 22-second mark, I heard him key the net.

"1, this is 2," he called.

"Go ahead 2."

"Roger, building clear, over."

"22 seconds, nice work," I told him.

"Roger. We have one male in custody with an RPK machine gun. What'd you say this guy's name was?"

I laughed. "You're fucking with me, right?"

"Naw, seriously, we've got a dude."

I still didn't believe him, but I pulled out my notebook and checked the name, relaying it to Barnes.

"Holy shit, we got him," he said, laughing.

And we had. When the front entry team hit the house, the man had been sprinting for the back door, but he opened it and ran smack into the six-foot bulk of Specialist Riley, who grabbed him by the neck and tossed him back inside. They secured the house and demanded his ID card, and sure enough, he was our target. Out of the hundreds of raids we had done, 95% had turned up empty – no one was home, or the target wasn't home but his family was, or we had the wrong house to begin with, but we almost *never* got the guy we were looking for. It was beyond absurd that during the most inane raid of the tour, designed more for training purposes than real tactical value, we had caught the right guy, with an illegal weapon, at home during the day. Chalk up another victory to pure dumb luck.

CHAPTER TWELVE

"All right, fellas: I would tell you not to do anything stupid
when we get back, but I know you will anyways,
so just don't fucking get caught."
-Staff Sergeant Barnes

The last days in Iraq seemed to rush by, for once – juggling patrols
and Movement Officer duties, I found myself fully occupied. But
when Valentine's Day rolled around, I managed to find a few minutes
to call my fiancée. As I walked back into our tent, I remembered
something Sergeant First Class Martin had told me earlier that day –
today was Staff Sergeant Barnes' birthday. I walked over to his cot,
where he was reading a worn paperback.

"Hey," I said, "Happy birthday, by the way."

"Mm-hm," he said, "Them assholes have already rolled me up for
it, too."

I laughed – apparently the platoon had jumped him and roughed
him up a bit as a birthday present. "What happened?"

"I was assaulted!" He said, indignantly. "By a gang of...of..."

"...hooligans?" I suggested.

"Hooligans, thank you, sir."

"Birthday on Valentine's Day, huh? That's kind of cool."

"Yeah...you would think that would get you a lot of pussy,"
Barnes told me. "But you'd be wrong. What really happens is that
two guaranteed pussy days turn into one."

I laughed, and went to drop my gear by my bunk. I was tired, or else I might have noticed the awkward silence in the tent, and some furtive glances from my soldiers. By the time they rushed me, it was too late. I fought them, laughing, but they easily overpowered me and thumped me for a while until Barnes called them off, although not before getting in a final good punch himself. I could feel a slight black eye coming on, though I couldn't for the life of me remember how I got it.

"You fuckers!" I yelled, still laughing.

Later, I called them together.

"Look, I want to thank you guys…"

"…don't think I've ever been *thanked* for rolling someone up," Sergeant Newsome noted.

"Shut up, Zach." I grinned at him. "I want to thank you guys for giving me the chance to lead you. It, uh…" I stumbled, searching for the right words. "…it really was an honor. I wouldn't want to go into combat with any other group of guys. That doesn't come close to describing how I feel, but it'll have to do."

We shook hands, smiling quietly. Once you've put your life into someone else's hands, other relationships pale in comparison, and we knew once we left this place, things would not be the same. Heading home was turning out to be unexpectedly bittersweet.

"One last thing: be careful tomorrow, and get home safe. I'll see you guys in Schweinfurt," I told them.

*   *   *

The following day, most of Bulldawg Troop convoyed their way down to the nearest logistics base, while I stayed behind to ensure our remaining equipment was properly shipped off. With only a dozen troopers left, we were officially done running missions: 1-15 Infantry was in charge, and the relief-in-place was officially complete. Knowing I would not be going out on mission again was a liberating feeling – I had survived my Iraq tour, and barring any freak occurrences on the trip itself, I should make it home in one piece. The relief was palpable. I supervised the loading of the last trailer of our equipment, tagged it with a satellite transponder, and watched as a massive crane lifted it onto a flatbed trailer. Then, with nothing official left to do, I caught up on some emails and some sleep, relaxing for the last couple of days before our flight south. But, as usual, Iraq had a surprise in store for me.

It happened because of an accident near Balad. A patrol from the unit that replaced 1-77 Armor managed to flip a Humvee into a canal, drowning all four crewmembers. The rumor was that they were operating in an area that 1-77 Armor had unofficially deemed unsafe for driving, and so 1st Infantry Division issued a new directive: while 1st Infantry Division soldiers remained in theater, they would accompany any and all 3rd Infantry Division patrols going out to prevent future such accidents. We were scheduled to fly out only two days later, but between now and then, Crusader Company from Task Force 1-15 would be running another patrol to the checkpoints outside Samarra. Ryan Simms and I got the news from Captain Hoffman the evening before they were scheduled to head out on patrol.

"...so one of you is going to have to accompany them," Hoffman said.

We looked at each other, shrugging, and to his great credit, Simms spoke up before me.

"I'll go," he said simply.

"You sure?" I asked. "I don't care." I didn't, really – it was just one more mission out of hundreds, regardless of being the day before we flew home.

"Yeah, I got it," Ryan told me. "I'm bored to death sitting around this tent anyways." Such is the selflessness of friends in combat.

"Okay," Hoffman said, "Ryan goes."

He left the following morning at dawn, one last trip out to the checkpoints where he had spent so much of the last few months. As I was sitting around later that morning, watching another DVD, Hoffman came into the tent.

"Lieutenant Platt," he said.

I pulled off my headphones, "Sir?"

"Crusader's got a broke-down tank out at FOB Rex – they're sending a recovery patrol out to pick it up and drop off a working tank."

I took a deep breath and reached for my uniform shirt. "Roger. Are they leaving now?"

"Yeah, they're waiting for you by the Squadron command post."

For my final patrol I would be riding in the loader's hatch of a Crusader Company tank, with a second tank as our wingman. I jogged down to the main road, spotting the two tanks idling by the refuel point. I clambered aboard with practiced ease, hopping into the loader's hatch next to the tank commander, Staff Sergeant Beale.

"Sorry we had to drag you along, sir," he yelled over the roar of the engines.

"That's okay," I told him, "I was starting to miss going out on missions."

"Really?" He asked, surprised.

"Fuck no," I replied. Beale grinned.

Not surprisingly, the tank was devoid of spare equipment, and I would have to wear my helmet and not the usual tank helmet with its ear-cups and microphone for communicating with the rest of the crew. Riding in a tank for several hours was going to be a noisy affair without the usual ear-cups, however, so I decided to put my earplugs in.

As we moved toward the front gate, I tended to the loader's M240 machine gun, my primary weapon for the mission. It was missing a hand-grip, which I pointed out to Staff Sergeant Beale.

"Sorry, sir – we don't have one."

I shrugged and took out some spare parachute cord, which I tied in a small loop around the trigger – it was a poor substitute, but it would work if I held the mount with one hand and pulled back on the loop with the other. I loaded it, set it to "SAFE," and then unlocked the mount, swinging the freed weapon along the full arc of its guide-rail as a final test.

The ride out to FOB Rex was both dusty and lonely, the unfamiliar crew largely leaving me alone, since conversation was so difficult without a tank helmet. I watched them maneuver their tanks ably, grumbling to myself at how unnecessary my presence was – even if I had needed to, giving them advice was nearly impossible since I wasn't on the intercom system or radio. I focused on routine security tasks instead, instinctively scanning the sides of the roads for IEDs, gesturing to Iraqi drivers to keep their distance when necessary, and otherwise operating on auto-pilot, the dull clanking of the tank treads muted in my ears.

After we passed the Iraqi Army barracks building a few miles south of FOB Mackenzie's entrance gate, Staff Sergeant Beale gestured to me and I leaned in close.

"Radio report says there was an IED back there by the barracks," he shouted, pushing aside his microphone.

"I didn't see it," I told him.

He shook his head – he hadn't, either. Later, EOD did find an IED on the stretch of road we had just passed, and detonated it: one more in a long string of close calls. We had to take the long way round to FOB Rex, rather than heading straight there off-road, as the shortcut route was still closed off with standing water and deep mud from the winter "rainy" season. We took the southern route to Samarra, instead, then cut north past the city, before looping back east towards FOB Rex.

FOB Rex was located on Route Grape, where numerous IEDs had struck Squadron units over the past year. I had driven the route enough times that it wasn't particularly nerve-wracking, but all the same, I couldn't help but think of the two soldiers from Bulldawg Troop who had lost their lives here earlier in the rotation, and the IED that had detonated near my own Humvee on an earlier patrol. As we came in sight of FOB Rex, we passed through an area where there were two high earthen berms on either side of the road. I thought to myself: *I remember this spot...I always thought it was a nasty choke point. I'm surprised they never hit us here.*

No sooner had I finished the thought when a massive explosion rocked the tank, debris and dirt showering us. The slap of the blast was so forceful that my arm felt like it had been slammed with a baseball bat. I had read about shell-shock among soldiers under artillery bombardment in the First and Second World Wars, but until you experience a blast of that magnitude up close, you can't really comprehend what it feels like. Apart from the obvious physical sensations – temporary loss of hearing, being tossed like a leaf in the wind, blinded by dust – it's like waking up suddenly in a strange place, trying to regain your bearings and remember what it is you were supposed to be doing. My first coherent thought was that I had been hit, and I immediately dropped down into the turret and patted myself down, checking for sharp pain or bleeding. Everything seemed to be alright, so I climbed back into position, grabbing the machine gun and swinging it through a full arc, scanning for moving vehicles or other suspicious activity. I saw nothing. I turned to Staff Sergeant Beale in the tank commander's hatch, who had a shocked look on his face and was speaking swiftly into his boom mike.

"You okay?" I yelled.

"Yeah!" He had evidently been talking to the driver, because we picked up speed and sped out of the area, heading towards FOB Rex, a few hundred yards down the road.

"Rest of the crew?"

Beale yelled again, "They're okay, sir!"

"You see any vehicle movement out there, or anything else?"

"No sir, I didn't see shit."

We didn't stop until we were at FOB Rex. The Crusader Company guys there had seen it happen, and they met us outside the fortifications, eyes wide.

"Holy shit!"

"That thing was fucking huge!"

"We just done popped our cherry!" Staff Sergeant Beale announced to the gawkers, obviously a little punch-drunk from the adrenaline rush.

I climbed down to take a look at the tank. There were minor shrapnel scratches here and there, and all of the tank's storage boxes had their lids blown open, but otherwise, there were no signs of major damage. The blast had somehow flipped my rifle through a complete 180 degrees; lying on the top of the tank, it was now facing in the opposite direction. On closer inspection, I saw that it had also acquired some deep scratches from the violence of being tossed about. There were rocks and dirt over everything, including my gear and uniform. I brushed myself off.

Staff Sergeant D'Angelo, one of my soldiers from Red Platoon who had been out at FOB Rex with the Crusader soldiers, walked up and clapped me on the back.

"You alright, sir?"

"Yeah...got all my arms and legs, nothing bleeding."

He nodded. "That fucking thing shook *the whole tank* I was sitting on. All the way back here! We're almost a kilometer away, for chrissakes."

"Jesus."

I was amazed at the lack of damage, considering the size of the IED – it was the biggest I'd seen in our tour, far larger than the two I had already experienced, and on the same scale as the one that had killed a tank driver in Anvil Troop, crushing the vehicle around him. It was a miracle we were all alive and the tank was in working condition. I certainly would have had long-term hearing damage had

I not been wearing my earplugs. The Crusader tank platoon leader walked up to me, shaking his head.

"This is your last mission, right?"

"Yeah," I told him wryly, "Which is good, because I think I just used up the last of my luck."

"Got that right," he said.

Once we had ensured it was working properly, our tank stayed onsite, and the second tank hooked up to the broken tank – the reason we'd come out in the first place – to tow it in. It hadn't occurred to me until that point, but I realized that we would be driving back to Mackenzie with just those two tanks linked together – one tank towing the broken tank, on which I would be riding. This arrangement wouldn't have flown in 1st Infantry Division; our policy was that you needed at least two operational vehicles at all times for safety. To have just a single working vehicle – which was severely handicapped because it was towing another – made me uncomfortable, but there was nothing I could do about it now.

As soon as the tanks were hooked up, we departed, retracing our route past the site of the IED attack. It was an even more massive hole than I had expected: half of the two-lane road was missing, and when they measured it later they found that it was eight feet deep and twelve feet across. Rather than bury the explosives, the insurgent had chosen to stuff them into a drainage pipe which passed underneath the road there, which is why we had seen no tell-tale IED signs ahead of time. It may just have been the reason we survived, as well – buried a solid five or six feet underground, most of the blast was contained by the earth above, though Staff Sergeant Beale had still been hit in the helmet with a large chunk of asphalt. I made it a point to scan my sector from lower down in my hatch, exposing as little of myself as possible.

Night had fallen by the time we passed back through Ad Montessim, when suddenly the tank towing us slowed to a crawl.

"What's up?" I asked Beale.

He spoke into his radio for a second, then shook his head ruefully.

"Goddamn tank just went into protective mode," he told me.

When they overheat or sensors determine a more major failure is imminent, tank engines are designed to enter "protective mode:" the engine's power is severely limited and the tank can do no more than crawl along at walking speed. This is usually a sign that the tank needs some serious repairs, but occasionally it's merely an electrical problem and the engine is actually fine. Standard operating procedure is to stop the tank, complete a full shutdown, and restart the engine to see if she'll come out of protective mode, just like rebooting a computer. In the tank ahead of us, the driver pushed the shutdown button. Nothing happened. Tanks fail to start up sometimes, but I'd never seen one refuse to *shut down*.

After several more attempts, they pulled the emergency fuel cutoff switch, which got the engine to stop, but apparently that wasn't such a good idea, because after pausing a few minutes to let her cool down, she wouldn't start up again. We were stranded, two broken tanks and eight soldiers, 20 miles from the nearest friendly unit, at night in enemy territory. About the only good news was that our radios still worked, so we promptly called for recovery support.

There were no recovery assets at FOB Mackenzie, so we would have to be rescued by the tanks we had just left out at the checkpoints, ironically. While they spooled up and headed out to us, Task Force 1-15 headquarters sent its quick reaction force Humvees and a Kiowa patrol out to secure us, apparently agreeing with my sentiment that having two broken tanks stranded outside the wire was a precarious situation. More than an hour later, the tanks arrived. After we had hooked both broken tanks up to be towed, we started off again.

Staff Sergeant Beale leaned over to me. "Well, I gotta say, sir – you've been pretty upbeat today considering all the crap we put you through."

"I'm going home, Sergeant – it's the only thing keeping me sane."

I knew, however, that our presence had not gone unnoticed, and we had been stuck out there more than enough time for an insurgent to set an IED along our route back to the FOB.

"Staff Sergeant Beale."

"Sir?"

"Where are the Kiowas going?"

"Back to base, sir – now that we're on our way in."

"I'm going to give you some advice, then – tell them to fly back to Mackenzie along our route. They can look for IEDs and spot anyone waiting to ambush us off the sides of the road. We were sitting out here a long time."

"Roger, good idea, sir."

I nodded – 13 months had taught us never to waste an air asset. The final leg home was slow and hot, the towing tank's exhaust washing over us in the dusty night. Finally, nearly nine hours after we had left, we returned to Mackenzie. I grabbed some midnight chow and returned to our tent, where Ryan Simms was already back from his own mission.

Captain Hoffman saw me first, laughing and clapping me on my back. "Welcome back, Platt! You're done – you're not going out again."

I wasn't in an exuberant mood. "Thanks, sir."

"What a last mission, huh?" Simms asked, shaking his head in disbelief.

"I couldn't have scripted it any better if I tried," I told him.

"Yeah. Let's get the fuck out of here, man."

EPILOGUE

It has been nine years, but some of Iraq is still with me. Unexpected loud noises still bother me – I jump embarrassingly when a car door is slammed or a heavy box is dropped, my body still trying to tell me that such things are threats. It took me a while to stop scanning the sides of the road looking for IEDs while I was in a car, and I still catch myself evaluating places from a tactical perspective: sizing up terrain, noting the entry and exit points, or where the most likely ambush might be.

Not all of it is bad: 13 months of having to know exactly where I was in a foreign land ingrained in me a deep, almost instinctual navigational awareness. I was in Paris on business, and after we checked into our hotel, my colleague and I decided to head towards the Champs-Élysées in search of a restaurant for dinner. I knew he had lived in Paris for a year, so I let him lead the way, but my subconscious started screaming at me immediately after we left the hotel – we were going the wrong way. After a block, I finally told him.

"Are you sure?" he asked.

"Yes," I said.

"Why?"

I thought about it for a second, realizing I hadn't reached this awareness consciously.

"We drove past the Champs-Élysées on the ride to the hotel," I told him, "but we're walking in the same direction we were last headed in the car. Plus, the Arc de Triomphe is on top of a small rise, and we're moving downhill now."

I have one recurring nightmare, though I don't think it stems from any of the more traumatic events I experienced. I am in unfriendly territory, and though I am calm and confident, when the enemy appears, none of my weapons work. I pull the trigger time and again, with no effect, becoming more and more frustrated while the anonymous enemy taunts me with a silent grin. It's not a grisly or horrific dream, just unsettling. I suppose it is a metaphor for our entire experience in Iraq, but I am too tired to appreciate the symbolism in the dark of the night.

Trying to summarize my experiences is difficult, partly because there was nothing conclusive or absolute about Iraq. I'm almost ashamed of my time in Iraq, compared to the experience of other veterans in history – it wasn't like the accounts I have read of Vietnam, or World War II, it wasn't epic or particularly life-changing or at all typical of the wars I had studied. I was attacked a number of times, had a handful of close brushes with death, and killed one unknown enemy from several hundred yards' distance, but otherwise spent most of the tour bored and frustrated, and returned unscathed. That's not to generalize for all those who have served in Iraq – I know there are soldiers who wish their experience had been a lot less traumatic, many in my own unit. I am grateful for having avoided that, but I feel unfulfilled, like a minor-leaguer who never gets his at-bat in the big leagues. I've been there, and I've done that, but...not in the way I expected.

Before we even left for Iraq, it had been fairly clear that we would have few strategic victories. Instead of going over there with the expectation of "winning," therefore, our commanders told us that "victory" would mean doing our job for a year, and doing it without casualties. At the time, we knew the latter goal would likely be unattainable, but I still resolved to do everything I could to bring all of my soldiers home, alive and uninjured. I hope that my actions as their leader played a small part in achieving that goal in my platoons, though I know it was mostly due to luck and the professionalism of my soldiers and NCOs. We made a difference to some Iraqis, to be sure – the election was a success, and I'm proud to have had a role in that. But the personal satisfaction of safely bringing every one of my soldiers home far outweighed anything else I had accomplished.

Other platoons were not so lucky. We talk of selfless sacrifice, of duty and courage, because these concepts somehow seem to ease the pain of their passing, and in some small way seem to justify the loss. But in the grand scheme of things, we ousted a brutal but stable dictatorship and replaced it with bitter sectarian violence, and the United States is no safer now than we were before we invaded Iraq. As a soldier who fought and lost friends there, I hope their deaths will serve as a deterrent to future generations, a warning of the consequences of ill-considered foreign interventions. But as a student of history, I'm not that naïve.

ABOUT THE AUTHOR

Piers Platt grew up in Boston, but spent most of his childhood in various boarding schools, including getting trained as a classical singer at a choir school for boys. He graduated from the University of Pennsylvania and joined the Army in 2002, spending four years on active duty. He lives with his wife and daughter in New York.

Back cover photos used with permission, courtesy of the United States Department of Defense. Use of military imagery does not imply or constitute endorsement of this book by the United States Department of Defense.